FREE
audio files to accompany this title can be accessed at
www.hoddergibson.co.uk

- Click on the blue 'Updates and Extras' box.
- Click on the relevant title.
- Click on 'Audio files': you will then find the files listed by year and question number.

INTERMEDIATE 2

FRENCH
2009-2013

HODDER GIBSON
LEARN MORE

Hodder Gibson is grateful to the copyright holders, as credited on the final page of the book, for permission to use their material. Every effort has been made to trace the copyright holders and to obtain their permission for the use of copyright material. Hodder Gibson will be happy to receive information allowing us to rectify any error or omission in future editions.

Hachette UK's policy is to use papers that are natural, renewable and recyclable products and made from wood grown in sustainable forests. The logging and manufacturing processes are expected to conform to the environmental regulations of the country of origin.

Orders: please contact Bookpoint Ltd, 130 Park Drive, Abingdon, Oxon OX14 4SE. Telephone: (44) 01235 827720. Fax: (44) 01235 400454.

Lines are open 9.00–5.00, Monday to Saturday, with a 24-hour message answering service. Visit our website at www.hoddereducation.co.uk. Hodder Gibson can be contacted direct on: Tel: 0141 848 1609; Fax: 0141 889 6315; email: hoddergibson@hodder.co.uk

This collection first published in 2013 by

Hodder Gibson, an imprint of Hodder Education,

An Hachette UK Company

2a Christie Street

Paisley PA1 1NB

BrightRED PUBLISHING Hodder Gibson is grateful to Bright Red Publishing Ltd for collaborative work in preparation of this book and all SQA Past Paper and National 5 Model Paper titles 2013.

Past Papers © Scottish Qualifications Authority. Answers and Study Skills section © Hodder Gibson. All rights reserved. Apart from any use permitted under UK copyright law, no part of this publication may be reproduced or transmitted in any form or by any means, electronic or mechanical, including photocopying and recording, or held within any information storage and retrieval system, without permission in writing from the publisher or under licence from the Copyright Licensing Agency Limited. Further details of such licences (for reprographic reproduction) may be obtained from the Copyright Licensing Agency Limited, Saffron House, 6–10 Kirby Street, London EC1N 8TS.

Typeset by PDQ Digital Media Solutions Ltd, Bungay, Suffolk NR35 1BY

Printed in the UK

A catalogue record for this title is available from the British Library

ISBN 978-1-4718-0251-5

3 2 1

2014 2013

Introduction

Study Skills – what you need to know to pass exams!

Pause for thought

Many students might skip quickly through a page like this. After all, we all know how to revise. Do you really though?

Think about this:

"IF YOU ALWAYS DO WHAT YOU ALWAYS DO, YOU WILL ALWAYS GET WHAT YOU HAVE ALWAYS GOT."

Do you like the grades you get? Do you want to do better? If you get full marks in your assessment, then that's great! Change nothing! This section is just to help you get that little bit better than you already are.

There are two main parts to the advice on offer here. The first part highlights fairly obvious things but which are also very important. The second part makes suggestions about revision that you might not have thought about but which WILL help you.

Part 1

DOH! It's so obvious but …

Start revising in good time

Don't leave it until the last minute – this will make you panic.

Make a revision timetable that sets out work time AND play time.

Sleep and eat!

Obvious really, and very helpful. Avoid arguments or stressful things too – even games that wind you up. You need to be fit, awake and focused!

Know your place!

Make sure you know exactly **WHEN and WHERE** your exams are.

Know your enemy!

Make sure you know what to expect in the exam.

How is the paper structured?

How much time is there for each question?

What types of question are involved?

Which topics seem to come up time and time again?

Which topics are your strongest and which are your weakest?

Are all topics compulsory or are there choices?

Learn by DOING!

There is no substitute for past papers and practice papers – they are simply essential! Tackling this collection of papers and answers is exactly the right thing to be doing as your exams approach.

Part 2

People learn in different ways. Some like low light, some bright. Some like early morning, some like evening / night. Some prefer warm, some prefer cold. But everyone uses their BRAIN and the brain works when it is active. Passive learning – sitting gazing at notes – is the most INEFFICIENT way to learn anything. Below you will find tips and ideas for making your revision more effective and maybe even more enjoyable. What follows gets your brain active, and active learning works!

Activity 1 – Stop and review

Step 1

When you have done no more than 5 minutes of revision reading STOP!

Step 2

Write a heading in your own words which sums up the topic you have been revising.

Step 3

Write a summary of what you have revised in no more than two sentences. Don't fool yourself by saying, 'I know it but I cannot put it into words'. That just means you don't know it well enough. If you cannot write your summary, revise that section again, knowing that you must write a summary at the end of it. Many of you will have notebooks full of blue/black ink writing. Many of the pages will not be especially attractive or memorable so try to liven them up a bit with colour as you are reviewing and rewriting. **This is a great memory aid, and memory is the most important thing.**

Activity 2 — Use technology!

Why should everything be written down? Have you thought about 'mental' maps, diagrams, cartoons and colour to help you learn? And rather than write down notes, why not record your revision material?

What about having a text message revision session with friends? Keep in touch with them to find out how and what they are revising and share ideas and questions.

Why not make a video diary where you tell the camera what you are doing, what you think you have learned and what you still have to do? No one has to see or hear it but the process of having to organise your thoughts in a formal way to explain something is a very important learning practice.

Be sure to make use of electronic files. You could begin to summarise your class notes. Your typing might be slow but it will get faster and the typed notes will be easier to read than the scribbles in your class notes. Try to add different fonts and colours to make your work stand out. You can easily Google relevant pictures, cartoons and diagrams which you can copy and paste to make your work more attractive and **MEMORABLE**.

Activity 3 – This is it. Do this and you will know lots!

Step 1

In this task you must be very honest with yourself! Find the SQA syllabus for your subject (www.sqa.org.uk). Look at how it is broken down into main topics called MANDATORY knowledge. That means stuff you MUST know.

Step 2

BEFORE you do ANY revision on this topic, write a list of everything that you already know about the subject. It might be quite a long list but you only need to write it once. It shows you all the information that is already in your long-term memory so you know what parts you do not need to revise!

Step 3

Pick a chapter or section from your book or revision notes. Choose a fairly large section or a whole chapter to get the most out of this activity.

With a buddy, use Skype, Facetime, Twitter or any other communication you have, to play the game "If this is the answer, what is the question?". For example, if you are revising Geography and the answer you provide is "meander", your buddy would have to make up a question like "What is the word that describes a feature of a river where it flows slowly and bends often from side to side?".

Make up 10 "answers" based on the content of the chapter or section you are using. Give this to your buddy to solve while you solve theirs.

Step 4

Construct a wordsearch of at least 10 X 10 squares. You can make it as big as you like but keep it realistic. Work together with a group of friends. Many apps allow you to make wordsearch puzzles online. The words and phrases can go in any direction and phrases can be split. Your puzzle must only contain facts linked to the topic you are revising. Your task is to find 10 bits of information to hide in your puzzle but you must not repeat information that you used in Step 3. DO NOT show where the words are. Fill up empty squares with random letters. Remember to keep a note of where your answers are hidden but do not show your friends. When you have a complete puzzle, exchange it with a friend to solve each other's puzzle.

Step 5

Now make up 10 questions (not "answers" this time) based on the same chapter used in the previous two tasks. Again, you must find NEW information that you have not yet used. Now it's getting hard to find that new information! Again, give your questions to a friend to answer.

Step 6

As you have been doing the puzzles, your brain has been actively searching for new information. Now write a NEW LIST that contains only the new information you have discovered when doing the puzzles. Your new list is the one to look at repeatedly for short bursts over the next few days. Try to remember more and more of it without looking at it. After a few days, you should be able to add words from your second list to your first list as you increase the information in your long-term memory.

FINALLY! Be inspired...

Make a list of different revision ideas and beside each one write **THINGS I HAVE** tried, **THINGS I WILL** try and **THINGS I MIGHT** try. Don't be scared of trying something new.

And remember – "FAIL TO PREPARE AND PREPARE TO FAIL!"

Intermediate 2 French

The course

The Intermediate 2 qualification in French develops students' abilities in the four language skills of Speaking, Listening, Reading and Writing. The content of the course is drawn from three prescribed themes: Lifestyles, Education and Work, and the Wider World, which subdivide into 5 topic areas. These are the topics you will have studied in depth and these are the same topics which the examiners will use to test you in the final examination. When speaking, listening, reading and writing on these topics at Intermediate level, **the content** will deal with topical issues, factual information and some personal opinions, and **the language** you have to understand and use in French will be mainly straightforward and predictable but will contain a range and variety of vocabulary, verb tenses and grammatical structures.

How the course is graded

The grade you are finally awarded for Intermediate 2 French depends on three elements:

- the internal assessments you do in school or college (the "NABs") – these don't count towards the final grade, but you must have passed them before you can achieve a final grade
- your Speaking assessment – this is recorded and assessed by your teacher at the end of March and the mark is then submitted to SQA and counts for 30% of your final grade
- the three external assessments which you sit in May and which test Reading (30% of your final grade), Listening (20% of your final grade) and Writing (20% of your final grade). Making sure you are well prepared to give your best performance in these three external assessments is what this book is all about! So bon travail et bonne chance!

The exam

The following information and advice is intended to help you plan and prepare for the external examination at Intermediate 2 level. It is based on advice given by the Principal Examiner as to how candidates can best approach the different elements of the exam in order to achieve the best possible performance. The hints and tips are presented firstly on how best to approach the papers which test comprehension (Paper 1 Reading and Paper 2 Listening) and then Paper 3 which tests Writing. Try reading the hints and tips and then put them into practice by trying the relevant past paper!

Tips for Reading

1. **BEFORE** trying to work out the meaning of any text (but particularly the long text at Intermediate 2), always read the introduction to the passage and the questions. These are in English and give important information as to what the different parts of the passage are about and also the type of information you need to find in order to answer the questions.
2. Keep your use of the dictionary to a minimum. You won't have time to look up every word and **the dictionary is not a substitute for learning key vocabulary! Target your revision of vocabulary** on the most common words from the prescribed themes of Lifestyles, Education and Work and the Wider World. Try using your knowledge of English, French vocabulary and French grammar to work out the meaning of any words that you don't immediately understand. Does the word look like an English word? E.g. "**participer**" = to participate/take part in. Does it look like a French word you know but is being used for a different grammatical purpose? E.g "**la pauvreté**" (noun) > "**pauvre**" (adjective) = poor > (the) poverty. However, also look out for "false friends" i.e. words which look like an English word but mean something else. Three of the most common ones are "**la journée**" (the day, not the journey which is "**le voyage**"), "**la lecture**" (reading) and "**L'Hôtel de ville**" (the town hall, not the town hotel).
3. The number of marks available for each question will **guide** you as to how much detail and information to include in your answers! Beware of guessing or including more items of information than you are asked for or you might be penalised under the "**extraneous rule**". The question usually indicates the amount of information you are required to give by stating in bold, e.g. "**Mention two of them**". If you then give three pieces of information and one is wrong and two are correct you may end up with only one mark instead of two.

Tips for Listening

1. As in the Reading exam, it is important to have revised vocabulary from the prescribed themes and topics, such as school subjects, places in town, things to eat and drink and leisure activities. It is also worth spending time revising numbers (times and prices), dates (days and months), weather expressions and seasons, as they should be easy to pick out from any listening text! Make sure that you pick up these "easier" points by recognising

numbers and time phrases such as "**15 heures par jour / de 9 heures à 13 / à 18 heures / la semaine dernière** (last) **/ l'été prochain** (next)" and directions such as "**nord/sud/ouest/est**". Many candidates also lose marks because they are unable to retain sufficient details required to accurately answer the questions, often understanding part of the information but not giving sufficient details, e.g. "**trois voitures et une moto / je vends des glaces / je répare les costumes**."

2. Before you hear the listening text for the first time, you will have time to look at the question paper and this will give you an indication of what you are about to hear. Use this time to anticipate the sort of French you might expect to hear given the context! In particular, look at each question and see what sort of information you will need to find, e.g. When? > time phrase / date etc. Where? > directions / preposition and place (e.g. "**devant la faculté**"). Use the number of marks available as a guide as to how much information you will need to find. **Don't** give more information than is required and **don't guess** and add information that you have not heard (**remember the extraneous rule!**)
3. Your answers don't need to be in sentences, but they must be clear and comprehensible. Be sure to score out any earlier notes and don't leave alternative answers because if one is right and one is wrong, you will end up with no marks!

Tips for Writing

1. To be at least "Satisfactory" your writing "must convey meaning clearly" which means you must be able to handle verbs accurately enough so that it is clear if the action is happening in the present, past or future. So be sure to practise handling the common verbs in these tenses! To gain a higher mark you will need to maintain a high level of grammatical accuracy and begin to write more complex sentences and use a greater range of vocabulary and structures. What you must avoid is making "serious basic errors" and introducing "mother tongue interference" through thinking in English and misusing the dictionary.
2. **Paper 3: Writing.** At Intermediate 2, the task is entirely predictable in that you must write (in French) a letter of application for a job in France (120–150 words). The details of the job will change from year to year but what you are asked to include in your letter will not. You must include information on the five compulsory bullet points and you will be penalised if you fail to write something on each of these areas. So be sure you have practised writing on each area and in particular, make sure you can spell the school subjects correctly and know how to write some relevant questions, e.g. "**Combien d'argent est-ce que je vais gagner par semaine?**" You can also include information on the two optional bullet points but you do not need to include this information and you will **not** be penalised if you do not.
3. You are also provided with the correct ways of starting and finishing a formal letter, so make sure you copy this help correctly and complete the opening sentence, making sure you are applying for the job in the advert, e.g. "Suite à votre annonce, je me permets de poser ma candidature pour le poste **de serveur / d'animateur?**".
4. Those who get high marks usually include information about the two optional areas and use them to show an **ability to use a range of tenses** (present, past, future and conditional). They usually give information about a holiday or a school trip to France and part-time jobs and the personal qualities they have, e.g. "**fiable**" (reliable)/ "**travailleur/-euse**" (hard-working). They try to reuse learned material that they are confident in and only use the dictionary to check the accuracy, gender ("**le, la, les**") or spelling (accents).
5. Those who get low marks tend to give long lists of school subjects (often incorrectly spelled), are not well prepared to give reasons for their application and have difficulty forming comprehensible questions when requesting information about the job. These candidates often misuse the dictionary by inventing and translating sentences from English to French!

FINAL TIP

In all papers, but especially in the Writing Paper, **make sure your handwriting is legible!**

Good luck!

Remember that the rewards for passing Intermediate 2 French are well worth it! Your pass will help you get the future you want for yourself. In the exam, be confident in your own ability. If you're not sure how to answer a question, trust your instincts and just give it a go anyway. Keep calm and don't panic! GOOD LUCK!

INTERMEDIATE 2

2009

[BLANK PAGE]

FOR OFFICIAL USE

Mark

X059/201

NATIONAL QUALIFICATIONS 2009

FRIDAY, 22 MAY
9.00 AM – 10.10 AM

FRENCH INTERMEDIATE 2
Reading

Fill in these boxes and read what is printed below.

Full name of centre

Town

Forename(s)

Surname

Date of birth
Day Month Year

Scottish candidate number

Number of seat

When you are told to do so, open your paper and write your answers **in English** in the spaces provided.

You may use a French dictionary.

Before leaving the examination room you must give this book to the invigilator. If you do not, you may lose all the marks for this paper.

PB X059/201 6/7320

©

DO NOT WRITE IN THIS MARGIN

Points

1. On the Internet you read about a competition in which schools can win a place at a European seminar in Strasbourg.

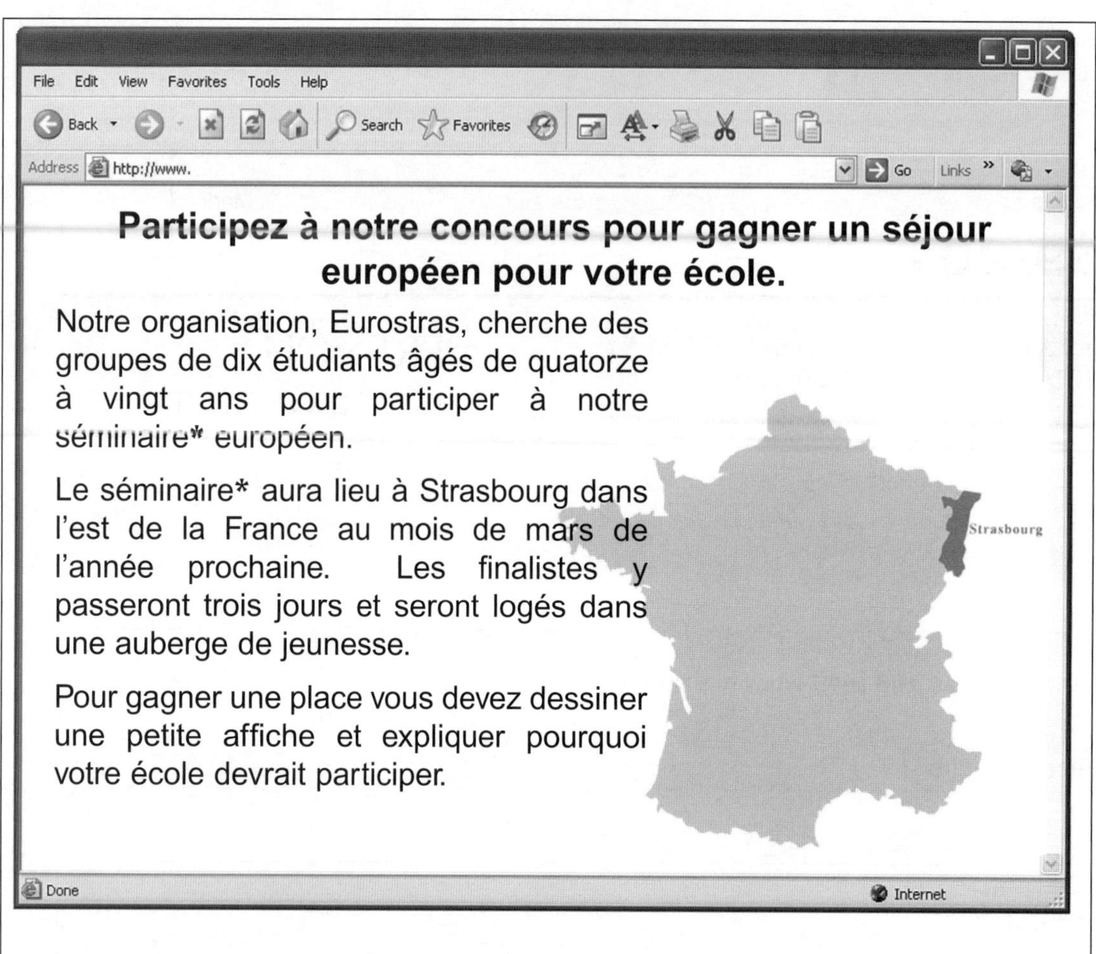

Participez à notre concours pour gagner un séjour européen pour votre école.

Notre organisation, Eurostras, cherche des groupes de dix étudiants âgés de quatorze à vingt ans pour participer à notre séminaire* européen.

Le séminaire* aura lieu à Strasbourg dans l'est de la France au mois de mars de l'année prochaine. Les finalistes y passeront trois jours et seront logés dans une auberge de jeunesse.

Pour gagner une place vous devez dessiner une petite affiche et expliquer pourquoi votre école devrait participer.

*** séminaire = seminar, conference**

(*a*) Complete the following sentence. **1**

The Eurostras organisation is looking for students aged between

________ and ________ .

(*b*) When will the seminar take place? Mention any **one** thing. **1**

____

(*c*) Where in Strasbourg will the finalists stay? **1**

____

(*d*) What do you have to do to win a place at the seminar? Mention **two** things. **2**

____

____

DO NOT WRITE IN THIS MARGIN

Points

2. You are very interested in the competition and you read on to find out more.

Premier jour
Tous les groupes se présentent en français et rencontrent les autres participants.

Deuxième jour
Chaque groupe va en ville pour vendre les produits traditionnels de son pays. Par exemple de la nourriture, des drapeaux ou des cartes postales.

Troisième jour
Une visite au Parlement, un bâtiment construit en verre, où les groupes discutent de la politique européenne.

A la fin des trois jours, le groupe qui a le mieux travaillé en équipe gagnera un prix de 500 Euros.

(*a*) What do the groups do on the first day? Mention any **one** thing. **1**

(*b*) Give any **two** examples of traditional products the groups might sell. **1**

(*c*) On the third day there is a visit to the European Parliament.

(i) What is the building like? **1**

(ii) What do the groups do during the visit? **1**

(*d*) Which group will win the prize? **1**

[Turn over

DO NOT WRITE IN THIS MARGIN

Points

3. You then read an article by Cédric, who was part of last year's winning group. He talks about his time in Strasbourg and what his school did with the money they won.

Mon séjour à Strasbourg

Le séjour à Strasbourg était génial. Pendant mon temps libre je me suis promené dans les rues de la ville et j'ai acheté des cadeaux pour ma famille. Le dernier soir tous les groupes ont fait la fête et nous avons chanté dans toutes les langues. J'étais un peu triste car je devais dire au revoir à mes nouveaux amis.

Notre groupe était content de gagner le prix. Nous avons utilisé l'argent pour créer un jardin dans notre école.

(*a*) What did Cédric do during his free time? Mention **two** things. **2**

____

____

(*b*) What happened on the last night? Mention any **one** thing. **1**

____

(*c*) Why was Cédric a little sad? **1**

____

(*d*) What did his group do with the prize money? **1**

____

[Turn over for Question 4 on *Pages six, seven* and *eight*

4. You read an article in a French magazine.

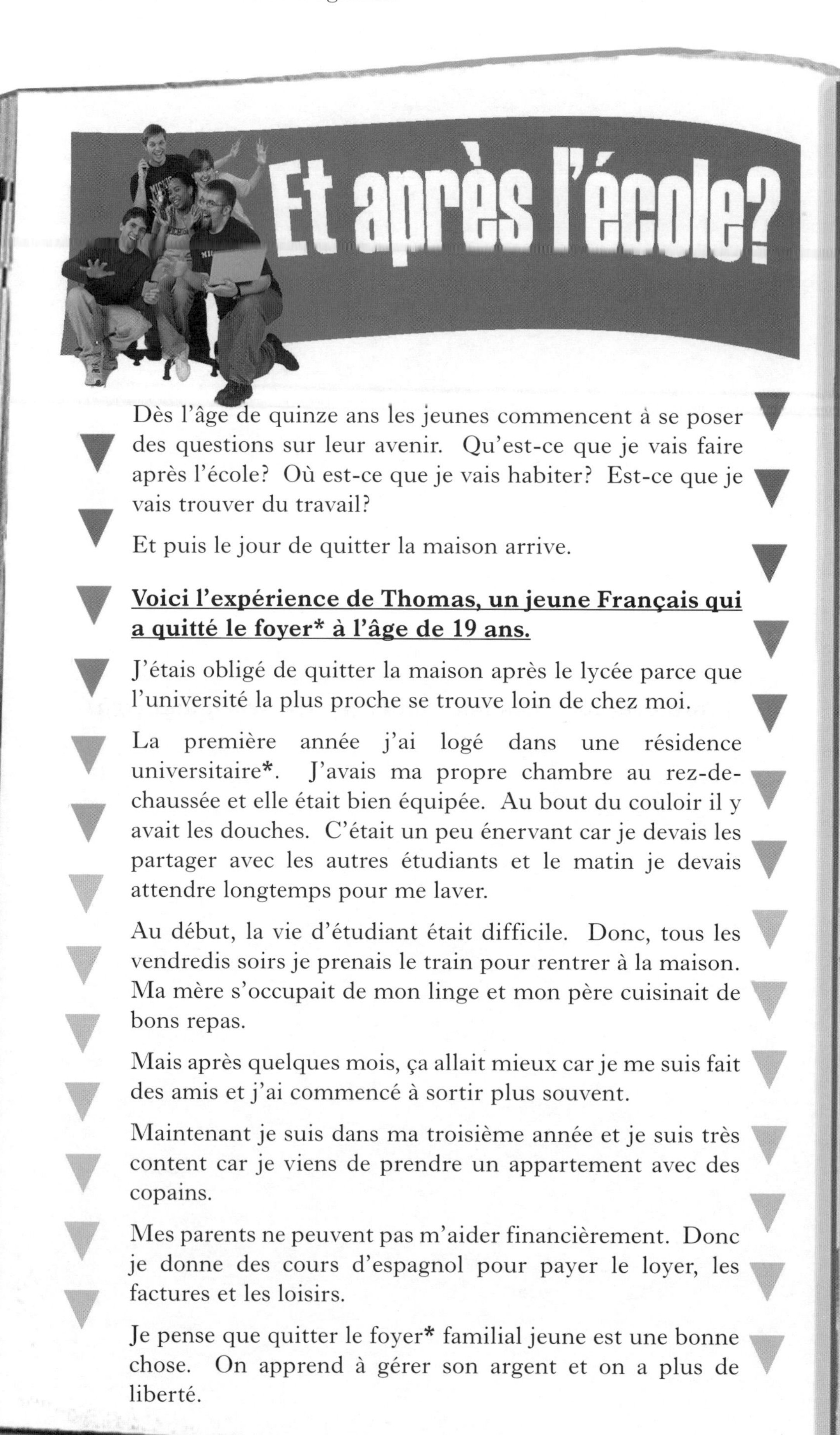

Et après l'école?

Dès l'âge de quinze ans les jeunes commencent à se poser des questions sur leur avenir. Qu'est-ce que je vais faire après l'école? Où est-ce que je vais habiter? Est-ce que je vais trouver du travail?

Et puis le jour de quitter la maison arrive.

Voici l'expérience de Thomas, un jeune Français qui a quitté le foyer* à l'âge de 19 ans.

J'étais obligé de quitter la maison après le lycée parce que l'université la plus proche se trouve loin de chez moi.

La première année j'ai logé dans une résidence universitaire*. J'avais ma propre chambre au rez-de-chaussée et elle était bien équipée. Au bout du couloir il y avait les douches. C'était un peu énervant car je devais les partager avec les autres étudiants et le matin je devais attendre longtemps pour me laver.

Au début, la vie d'étudiant était difficile. Donc, tous les vendredis soirs je prenais le train pour rentrer à la maison. Ma mère s'occupait de mon linge et mon père cuisinait de bons repas.

Mais après quelques mois, ça allait mieux car je me suis fait des amis et j'ai commencé à sortir plus souvent.

Maintenant je suis dans ma troisième année et je suis très content car je viens de prendre un appartement avec des copains.

Mes parents ne peuvent pas m'aider financièrement. Donc je donne des cours d'espagnol pour payer le loyer, les factures et les loisirs.

Je pense que quitter le foyer* familial jeune est une bonne chose. On apprend à gérer son argent et on a plus de liberté.

4. (continued) *Points* DO NOT WRITE IN THIS MARGIN

La mère de Thomas donne son point de vue.

Je me suis inquiétée quand Thomas a quitté la maison pour la première fois. J'avais peur qu'il ne mange pas correctement ou qu'il se perde dans une grande ville.

Mais heureusement tout va très bien et il m'appelle une fois par semaine pour me donner des nouvelles.

Si vous quittez la maison pour aller à l'université, je vous conseille de visiter la ville avant de faire un choix. Il est très important d'aimer l'endroit où vous allez passer quelques années.

*** le foyer = the household**
*** une résidence universitaire = halls of residence**

(*a*) According to the first paragraph young people ask themselves many questions about their future. Mention any **two**. 2

Thomas talks about his experience of leaving home to go to university.

(*b*) What does Thomas say about his room in the halls of residence? Mention any **two** things. 2

(*c*) What annoyed Thomas about the showers? Mention any **one** thing. 1

(*d*) At the beginning he went back home every Friday evening.

(i) What did his mum do for him? 1

(ii) What did his dad do? 1

DO NOT WRITE IN THIS MARGIN

Points

4. (continued)

(*e*) Why did things get better after a few months? Mention any **one** thing. 1

(*f*) Thomas' parents cannot help him financially.

(i) What does Thomas do to earn money? 1

(ii) What does he need this money for? Mention any **two** things. 2

(*g*) Why does he think it is a good thing to leave home at a young age? Mention any **one** thing. 1

Thomas' mother gives her point of view.

(*h*) What was Thomas' mother worried about when he left home? Mention any **one** thing. 1

(*i*) How does she know everything is fine? Mention **one** thing. 1

(*j*) Why does she advise young people to visit the town before choosing a university? 1

Total (30 points)

= 30 marks

[*END OF QUESTION PAPER*]

X059/203

NATIONAL QUALIFICATIONS 2009

FRIDAY, 22 MAY
10.30 AM – 11.00 AM
(APPROX)

FRENCH INTERMEDIATE 2
Listening Transcript

This paper must not be seen by any candidate.

The material overleaf is provided for use in an emergency only (eg the recording or equipment proving faulty) or where permission has been given in advance by SQA for the material to be read to candidates with additional support needs. The material must be read exactly as printed.

Transcript—Intermediate 2

Instructions to reader(s):

For each item, read the English **once**, then read the French **twice**, with an interval of 1 minute between the two readings. On completion of the second reading, pause for the length of time indicated in brackets after each item, to allow the candidates to write their answers.

Where special arrangements have been agreed in advance to allow the reading of the material, those sections marked **(f)** should be read by a female speaker and those marked **(m)** by a male: those sections marked **(t)** should be read by the teacher.

(t) You are attending a European seminar in Strasbourg.

Question number one.

Nadine, one of the other participants, tells you about her school.

You now have one minute to study the question.

(f) **Je fréquente un grand lycée international au centre de Genève en Suisse. Comme les élèves sont de toutes nationalités, les cours se font en anglais, sauf les cours de langues bien sûr. Moi, j'apprends l'allemand en langue étrangère. Je la trouve un peu difficile et en plus le prof est très ennuyeux. Je fais 7 matières au total mais ma matière préférée est le dessin. Je l'aime bien car ça m'aide à me détendre et à oublier mes problèmes. De plus je fais des dessins pour notre magazine scolaire qui paraît chaque trimestre. On y trouve aussi des articles sur les problèmes familiaux ou des conseils pour avoir de meilleures notes à l'école. Le magazine est vendu aux élèves, aux profs, aux parents et aux habitants de notre ville. Le magazine a un grand succès et fait un bon profit. On donne un peu de l'argent des ventes à une association qui aide les enfants pauvres.**

(*3 minutes*)

(t) **Question number two.**

Nadine then goes on to tell you about her holiday in Greece last year.

You now have one minute to study the question.

(f) **L'année dernière je suis partie avec mes amis pour quinze jours en Grèce. C'était la première fois que j'allais en vacances sans mes parents et j'étais à la fois excitée mais aussi un peu anxieuse. J'avais raison de l'être. Les problèmes ont commencé à l'aéroport. D'abord un de mes amis avait oublié son passeport. Ensuite l'avion avait 5 heures de retard à cause du brouillard. Quand on est enfin arrivé en Grèce, on a pris un taxi pour aller à notre villa. Elle était très sale et il n'y avait pas de frigo. Le reste de la première semaine s'est passé sans trop de problèmes. Il a fait super beau et on passait les journées à se baigner dans la piscine et à jouer aux cartes sur la terrasse. Et puis un jour on a décidé de louer des vélos. Quelle mauvaise idée! Moi, je suis tombée de vélo et je me suis cassé la jambe. On a été obligé de m'emmener à l'hôpital et c'est là-bas que j'ai passé le reste de mes vacances. C'était vraiment des vacances désastreuses.**

(*3 minutes*)

(t) Question number three.

While you are in Strasbourg, you listen to the radio. You hear a news item about a break-in at a big supermarket.

You now have one minute to study the question.

(m) Un grand hypermarché a été cambriolé cette nuit à trois heures du matin. L'hypermarché se trouve à 8 km de Strasbourg et est un des plus grands de la ville. Les 3 voleurs ont pris des vêtements, des ordinateurs et de l'alcool. La police croit que ces jeunes hommes doivent connaître quelqu'un qui travaille dans le magasin parce qu'ils sont entrés sans déclencher l'alarme. Ils ont été filmés par des caméras de surveillance et ont entre 18 et 24 ans. Ils sont tous de taille moyenne et étaient habillés en jean et pull noir avec des baskets blanches. Un des voleurs a les cheveux longs et blonds et porte des lunettes. Les 3 voleurs sont partis par le parking du sous-sol dans un camion vert. Ni le camion ni les voleurs n'ont été retrouvés. La police cherche des témoins. Si vous avez des informations veuillez appeler le 03-88-20-54-16.

(*3 minutes*)

(t) End of test.

Now look over your answers.

[*END OF TRANSCRIPT*]

[BLANK PAGE]

FOR OFFICIAL USE

Mark

X059/202

NATIONAL QUALIFICATIONS 2009

FRIDAY, 22 MAY
10.30 AM – 11.00 AM (APPROX)

FRENCH
INTERMEDIATE 2
Listening

Fill in these boxes and read what is printed below.

Full name of centre

Town

Forename(s)

Surname

Date of birth
Day Month Year

Scottish candidate number

Number of seat

When you are told to do so, open your paper.

You will hear three items in French. **Before you hear each item, you will have one minute to study the question.** You will hear each item twice, with an interval of one minute between playings, then you will have time to answer the questions about it before hearing the next item.

Write your answers, **in English**, in this book, in the appropriate spaces.

You may take notes as you are listening to the French, but only in this book.

You may **not** use a French dictionary.

You are not allowed to leave the examination room until the end of the test.

Before leaving the examination room you must give this book to the invigilator. If you do not, you may lose all the marks for this paper.

PB X059/202 6/7320

©

DO NOT WRITE IN THIS MARGIN

Points

You are attending a European seminar in Strasbourg.

1. Nadine, one of the other participants, tells you about her school.

(*a*) Where is Nadine's school? Mention any **one** thing. **1**

____

(*b*) Mention **two** things she says about learning German. **2**

____

____

(*c*) Why is art Nadine's favourite subject? Mention **two** things. **2**

____

____

(*d*) There is a magazine in her school. What are the articles about? Mention any **one** thing. **1**

____

____

(*e*) Who do they help with the money they make from the magazine? **1**

____

* * * * *

DO NOT WRITE IN THIS MARGIN

Points

2. Nadine then goes on to tell you about her holiday in Greece last year.

(*a*) How long did Nadine go on holiday for? **1**

(*b*) Their problems started at the airport.

(i) What was the first problem they had? **1**

(ii) Why was the plane late? **1**

(*c*) What problems did they have with their villa? Mention any **one** thing. **1**

(*d*) The rest of the week went well. What did they do during the day? Mention any **one** thing. **1**

(*e*) They decided to hire bikes. Why was this a bad idea? Mention any **two** things. **2**

* * * * *

[Turn over for Question 3 on *Page four*

DO NOT WRITE IN THIS MARGIN

Points

3. While you are in Strasbourg, you listen to the radio. You hear a news item about a break-in at a big supermarket.

(*a*) At what time did the break-in take place? 1

____

(*b*) What did the thieves steal? Mention any **two** things. 2

____

____

(*c*) What were the thieves wearing? Complete the following sentence. 1

They were wearing jeans, a black _______________ and

_______________ trainers.

(*d*) How did they escape? Mention any **one** thing. 1

____

(*e*) Complete the telephone number you should call if you have any information. 1

03–88–20–____ – ____

*   *   *   *   *

Total (20 points)
= 20 marks

[*END OF QUESTION PAPER*]

X059/204

NATIONAL QUALIFICATIONS 2009

FRIDAY, 22 MAY 11.20 AM – 12.00 NOON

FRENCH INTERMEDIATE 2

Writing

20 marks are allocated to this paper.

You may use a French dictionary.

You are preparing an application for the job advertised below.

Employeur:	**Hôtel IBIS – Strasbourg**
Poste:	Serveur/serveuse
Profil:	Responsable du service dans le restaurant de l'hôtel. Vous devez parler l'anglais et le français.
Renseignements:	Pour plus de détails sur les horaires, le salaire, l'hébergement etc. **Contactez** Hôtel IBIS **19, Place de la Cathédrale** **67000 Strasbourg, France**

To help you to write your application, you have been given the following checklist of information to give about yourself and to ask about the job. Make sure you deal with **all** of these points:

- name, age, where you live
- leisure interests
- school/college career – subjects studied previously/being studied now
- reasons for application
- request for information about the job.

You could also include the following information:

- any previous links with France or a French-speaking country
- work experience, if any.

You have also been given a way to start and finish this formal type of letter:

Formal opening to letter of application

> Monsieur/Madame/Messieurs,
>
> Suite à votre annonce, je me permets de poser ma candidature pour le poste de . . .

Formal finish to letter of application

> En espérant que ma demande retiendra votre attention, je vous prie d'accepter, Monsieur/Madame/Messieurs, l'expression de mes sentiments distingués.

Use all of the above to help you write **in French** the letter which should be 120–150 words, excluding the formal phrases you have been given. You may use a French dictionary.

[*END OF QUESTION PAPER*]

INTERMEDIATE 2

2010

[BLANK PAGE]

FOR OFFICIAL USE

Mark

X059/201

NATIONAL QUALIFICATIONS 2010

TUESDAY, 18 MAY 9.00 AM – 10.10 AM

FRENCH INTERMEDIATE 2 Reading

Fill in these boxes and read what is printed below.

Full name of centre

Town

Forename(s)

Surname

Date of birth

Day Month Year

Scottish candidate number

Number of seat

When you are told to do so, open your paper and write your answers **in English** in the spaces provided.

You may use a French dictionary.

Before leaving the examination room you must give this book to the Invigilator. If you do not, you may lose all the marks for this paper.

©

DO NOT WRITE IN THIS MARGIN

Marks

1. You want to take a year out to work in France. You see an advert on the Internet from a Senegalese family looking for an au pair to help look after their children.

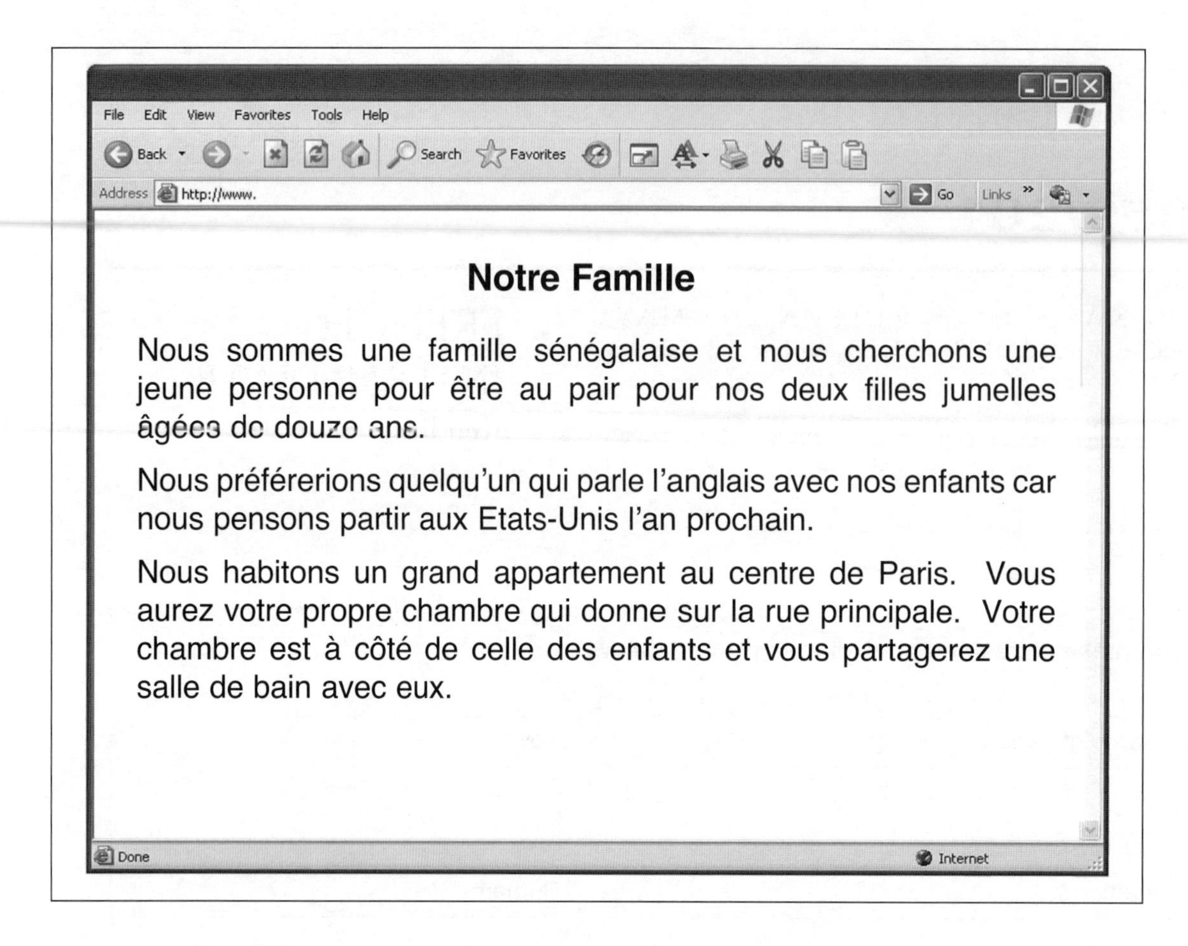

Notre Famille

Nous sommes une famille sénégalaise et nous cherchons une jeune personne pour être au pair pour nos deux filles jumelles âgées de douze ans.

Nous préférerions quelqu'un qui parle l'anglais avec nos enfants car nous pensons partir aux Etats-Unis l'an prochain.

Nous habitons un grand appartement au centre de Paris. Vous aurez votre propre chambre qui donne sur la rue principale. Votre chambre est à côté de celle des enfants et vous partagerez une salle de bain avec eux.

(*a*) Mention **two** things about the two girls in the family. **2**

(*b*) Why would the family prefer someone who speaks English? **1**

(*c*) What are you told about your living arrangements? Tick (✓) the **two** correct sentences. **2**

Your bedroom must be kept clean.	
You will have the main bedroom.	
Your bedroom is next to the children's.	
You will have to share the bathroom.	

DO NOT WRITE IN THIS MARGIN

Marks

2. You are interested and you read on to find out more about the job.

Le travail

Vous travaillerez tous les jours sauf le mercredi et le dimanche.

Vous aiderez les enfants à faire leurs devoirs et vous vous occuperez d'eux le soir si nous sortons.

Vous ferez de petits travaux ménagers comme le repassage ou aider à la préparation des repas.

Pendant vos jours de congé, vous pourrez suivre des cours de français ou aller vous promener dans les quartiers voisins.

(*a*) When will you have to work? **1**

(*b*) What will you have to do for the children? **2**

(*c*) What household tasks will you be expected to carry out? Mention any **one**. **1**

(*d*) What does the family suggest you could do on your days off? Mention any **one** thing. **1**

[Turn over

DO NOT WRITE IN THIS MARGIN

Marks

3. You have been successful in your application for the job. While in France the family shows you an article about Senegal, their home country, which is in West Africa.

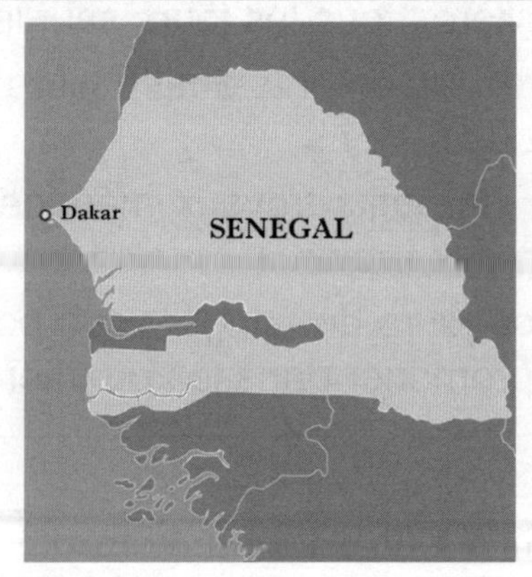

Le Sénégal était une colonie française et l'influence française y est vraiment sentie: la langue française est parlée partout et il existe encore des bâtiments historiques qui datent de cette époque là.

Le tourisme au Sénégal continue d'augmenter grâce au soleil qui brille pratiquement toute l'année et à l'accueil chaleureux de sa population. Le Sénégal offre beaucoup de choses aux touristes comme, par exemple, des côtes de toute beauté, des villages traditionnels de pêcheurs et des villes animées.

(*a*) Senegal was a French colony. How is the French influence still felt in Senegal? **2**

____

____

(*b*) Why is tourism continuing to increase in Senegal? Mention any **one** thing. **1**

____

(*c*) What does Senegal have to offer to tourists? Mention any **two** things. **2**

____

____

[Turn over for Question 4 on *Pages six, seven* and *eight*

4. You read an article in a magazine about holidays.

Les vacances arrivent!

Tout le monde a besoin de vacances pour oublier le travail ou les études et pour s'échapper de la vie quotidienne. Mais où faut-il aller pour passer des vacances idéales?

Deux personnes nous parlent de leurs vacances bien différentes.

Caroline

L'année dernière était une année très difficile pour moi. J'ai rompu avec mon copain puis j'ai été malade pendant quelques mois. J'ai donc décidé de partir une semaine en Espagne. Je ne voulais que me reposer en faisant un peu de lecture et de bronzage.

Le premier jour, j'ai décidé d'aller à la plage, mais quel désastre! Il y avait trop de monde, pas assez de place pour poser ma serviette et en plus, comme il faisait très chaud, j'ai pris un coup de soleil très douloureux.

Les soirées n'étaient pas mieux. La nourriture dans l'hôtel n'était pas bonne et je n'arrivais pas à dormir à cause du bruit des boîtes de nuit. De plus, il y avait des moustiques qui me piquaient sans cesse.

A la fin de la semaine je me sentais encore plus fatiguée et en fait, j'avais besoin de vacances en rentrant à la maison!

La famille Casse

Avant, notre famille n'aimait pas partir en vacances parce qu'on avait toujours peur de laisser la maison vide et il n'y avait personne pour arroser le jardin ou les fleurs. Mais un jour, on a lu un article dans un magazine qu'il était possible de faire un échange de maison. On s'est tout de suite renseigné et maintenant on part en vacances chaque année chez des gens, qui eux, viennent chez nous. C'est idéal pour notre famille. On a tout le confort d'une maison et on est loin des touristes. On fait aussi la connaissance des autres familles qui vivent dans les alentours et donc nos deux enfants ne s'ennuient jamais.

De plus, ces vacances ne sont pas chères car il n'y a qu'un billet d'avion et quelques frais d'agences à payer. Le seul inconvénient est qu'on doit faire le ménage avant de partir!

DO NOT WRITE IN THIS MARGIN

Marks

4. (continued)

(*a*) Why does everyone need a holiday? Mention any **one** thing. 1

Caroline

(*b*) Why had it been a difficult year for Caroline? Mention any **one** thing. 1

(*c*) Where and for how long did she go on holiday? 1

(*d*) What did she want to do on holiday? Mention any **two** things. 2

(*e*) Why was her first day at the beach a disaster? Mention any **two** things. 2

(*f*) What problems did she have in the evenings? Mention any **two** things. 2

DO NOT WRITE IN THIS MARGIN

Marks

4. (continued)

La famille Casse

(*g*) Why did the Casse family not like going on holiday? Mention any **one** thing. **1**

(*h*) How did they find out about the possibility of doing a house exchange? **1**

(*i*) Why is this type of holiday ideal for the Casse family? Mention any **three** things. **3**

(*j*) Why is this type of holiday not expensive? Mention any **one** thing. **1**

Total (30)

[*END OF QUESTION PAPER*]

X059/203

NATIONAL QUALIFICATIONS 2010

TUESDAY, 18 MAY
10.30 AM – 11.00 AM
(APPROX)

FRENCH
INTERMEDIATE 2
Listening Transcript

This paper must not be seen by any candidate.

The material overleaf is provided for use in an emergency only (eg the recording or equipment proving faulty) or where permission has been given in advance by SQA for the material to be read to candidates with additional support needs. The material must be read exactly as printed.

©

Transcript—Intermediate 2

Instructions to reader(s):

For each item, read the English **once**, then read the French **twice**, with an interval of 1 minute between the two readings. On completion of the second reading, pause for the length of time indicated in brackets after each item, to allow the candidates to write their answers.

Where special arrangements have been agreed in advance to allow the reading of the material, those sections marked **(f)** should be read by a female speaker and those marked **(m)** by a male: those sections marked **(t)** should be read by the teacher.

(t) You are working as an au pair for a family in France. One evening the family invites friends, Pauline and Bruno, to dinner.

Question number one.

Pauline tells you about a school trip she went on to England.

You now have one minute to study the question.

(f) **Quand j'avais 16 ans j'ai participé à un échange scolaire avec mon école. Nous avons passé un mois dans le sud de l'Angleterre avec une famille d'accueil. La famille était vraiment gentille et je me suis très bien entendue avec leur fille, Louise. Elle avait le même âge que moi et on avait les mêmes intérêts, surtout la mode. Tous les matins, j'allais à l'école avec Louise. Les cours de français étaient marrants. Le prof m'a demandé de parler en français de ma famille et de ma ville, c'était vraiment très intéressant. J'ai trouvé l'école très différente de mon lycée. En Grande-Bretagne, les profs sont plus compréhensifs et les élèves ont moins de devoirs. Je passais les soirées avec ma famille d'accueil et après le dîner, on jouait aux cartes ou on discutait des différences entre la France et l'Angleterre. J'ai vraiment adoré l'Angleterre et après ce séjour j'ai décidé d'étudier les langues étrangères.**

(3 minutes)

(t) Question number two.

Pauline goes on to tell you about the gap year she took after leaving school.

You now have one minute to study the question.

(f) **Après le lycée et avant de commencer à faire de longues études à la fac, j'ai décidé de prendre une année sabbatique et de voyager en Europe. Au début mes parents étaient contre parce qu'ils croyaient que j'étais trop jeune et qu'il était trop dangereux pour une jeune fille de voyager seule. Heureusement, ma tante qui vivait au Portugal a dit que je pourrais loger chez elle pendant quelque temps. Mes parents ont donc accepté à condition que je les contacte tous les jours et que j'aide ma tante à faire les tâches ménagères. Malheureusement, je me suis mal entendue avec ma tante. Je devais rentrer à 21 heures tous les soirs et je n'avais pas le droit d'inviter mes copains à la maison. Par conséquent, j'ai décidé de louer un appartement avec mes nouveaux amis. Pour payer le logement j'ai trouvé un petit boulot à la plage où je vendais des glaces. J'ai fini par passer toute l'année au Portugal. D'accord, je n'ai peut-être pas fait le tour de l'Europe mais j'ai eu ma première expérience de la vie sans mes parents et j'ai gagné beaucoup de confiance en moi.**

(3 minutes)

(t) **Question number three.**

Bruno talks about the voluntary work he did in Senegal, a country in Africa.

You now have one minute to study the question.

(m) **Moi aussi, j'ai travaillé à l'étranger. Je suis parti au Sénégal il y a un an pour participer à un projet de volontariat qui a duré 6 semaines. Mon projet était de travailler dans une école maternelle avec des enfants âgés de trois à six ans. Les enfants étaient fascinés par ma vie et je devais répondre à toutes leurs questions sur la France et l'Europe. Je devais aussi organiser toutes sortes d'activités pour stimuler l'intérêt des jeunes enfants, par exemple des jeux et des chansons. Les gens du Sénégal sont extraordinaires. Ils ont peu d'argent, donc en général ils sont très pauvres et pourtant ils sont toujours très souriants. Ce projet a vraiment changé ma vie. Depuis mon retour en France, je pense continuellement aux Sénégalais que j'ai rencontrés là-bas et j'ai déjà l'intention de repartir en fin d'année pour les retrouver. A mon avis, c'est en participant à un tel projet que l'on apprend vraiment à connaître un pays et ses habitants.**

(3 minutes)

(t) **End of test.**

Now look over your answers.

[*END OF TRANSCRIPT*]

[BLANK PAGE]

FOR OFFICIAL USE

X059/202

Mark

NATIONAL QUALIFICATIONS 2010

TUESDAY, 18 MAY
10.30 AM – 11.00 AM (APPROX)

FRENCH
INTERMEDIATE 2
Listening

Fill in these boxes and read what is printed below.

Full name of centre

Town

Forename(s)

Surname

Date of birth
Day Month Year

Scottish candidate number

Number of seat

When you are told to do so, open your paper.

You will hear three items in French. **Before you hear each item, you will have one minute to study the question.** You will hear each item twice, with an interval of one minute between playings, then you will have time to answer the questions about it before hearing the next item.

Write your answers, **in English**, in this book, in the appropriate spaces.

You may take notes as you are listening to the French, but only in this book.

You may **not** use a French dictionary.

You are not allowed to leave the examination room until the end of the test.

Before leaving the examination room you must give this book to the Invigilator. If you do not, you may lose all the marks for this paper.

©

DO NOT WRITE IN THIS MARGIN

Marks

You are working as an au pair for a family in France. One evening the family invites friends, Pauline and Bruno, to dinner.

1. Pauline tells you about a school trip she went on to England.

(*a*) How old was Pauline when she went on the school trip? **1**

(*b*) Why did Pauline and Louise get on well? **2**

(*c*) What did the French teacher ask her to talk about? Mention **two** things. **1**

(*d*) Pauline compares her school with those in Great Britain. What did she find different in British schools? Mention any **one** thing. **1**

(*e*) How did Pauline spend the evenings with the family after dinner? Mention any **one** thing. **1**

(*f*) What did Pauline decide to do after her trip to England? **1**

* * * * *

DO NOT WRITE IN THIS MARGIN

Marks

2. Pauline goes on to tell you about the gap year she took after leaving school.

(*a*) Why were her parents against her taking a gap year? Mention any **one** thing. **1**

(*b*) Pauline's aunt in Portugal offered to let Pauline stay. On what conditions was she allowed to stay with her aunt? Mention any **one.** **1**

(*c*) Unfortunately, Pauline did not get on with her aunt.

(i) Mention any **one** reason she gives for this. **1**

(ii) What happened as a result of these problems? **1**

(*d*) What job did Pauline find in Portugal? **1**

(*e*) What did Pauline gain from her year in Portugal? Mention any **one** thing. **1**

* * * * *

[Turn over for Question 3 on *Page four*

DO NOT WRITE IN THIS MARGIN

Marks

3. Bruno talks about the voluntary work he did in Senegal, a country in Africa.

(*a*) When did Bruno go to Senegal? **1**

____

(*b*) What did the project involve? Complete the sentence. **2**

He worked in a ________________ with children between __________

and __________ years old.

(*c*) Mention any **one** activity Bruno had to organise. **1**

____

(*d*) Why did he find the people of Senegal extraordinary? **2**

____

____

(*e*) What does Bruno say you learn by taking part in such a project? **1**

____

* * * * *

Total (20)

[*END OF QUESTION PAPER*]

X059/204

NATIONAL QUALIFICATIONS 2010

TUESDAY, 18 MAY 11.20 AM – 12.00 NOON

FRENCH INTERMEDIATE 2

Writing

20 marks are allocated to this paper.

You may use a French dictionary.

You are preparing an application for the job advertised below.

Poste:	Aide de bureau. Nous recherchons une personne responsable pour • répondre au téléphone • classer des documents
Profil:	Il faut avoir de bonnes aptitudes d'organisation, la connaissance d'une langue étrangère et être capable de bien travailler avec les autres.
Renseignements:	Pour plus de détails sur les horaires, le salaire etc. contactez: **Madame TEMMIN** Agence Auban 25 rue du Taur Toulouse 31000 France

To help you to write your application, you have been given the following checklist of information to give about yourself and to ask about the job. Make sure you deal with **all** of these points:

- name, age, where you live
- leisure interests
- school/college career – subjects studied previously/being studied now
- reasons for application
- request for information about the job.

You could also include the following information:

- any previous links with France or a French-speaking country
- work experience, if any.

You have also been given a way to start and finish this formal type of letter:

Formal opening to letter of application

Monsieur/Madame/Messieurs,

Suite à votre annonce, je me permets de poser ma candidature pour le poste de . . .

Formal finish to letter of application

En espérant que ma demande retiendra votre attention, je vous prie d'accepter, Monsieur/Madame/Messieurs, l'expression de mes sentiments distingués.

Use all of the above to help you write **in French** the letter which should be 120–150 words, excluding the formal phrases you have been given. You may use a French dictionary.

[*END OF QUESTION PAPER*]

INTERMEDIATE 2

2011

HODDER GIBSON
LEARN MORE

[BLANK PAGE]

FOR OFFICIAL USE

Mark

X059/201

NATIONAL QUALIFICATIONS 2011

TUESDAY, 17 MAY
9.00 AM – 10.10 AM

FRENCH INTERMEDIATE 2
Reading

Fill in these boxes and read what is printed below.

Full name of centre

Town

Forename(s)

Surname

Date of birth
Day Month Year

Scottish candidate number

Number of seat

When you are told to do so, open your paper and write your answers **in English** in the spaces provided.

You may use a French dictionary.

Before leaving the examination room you must give this book to the Invigilator. If you do not, you may lose all the marks for this paper.

©

DO NOT WRITE IN THIS MARGIN

Marks

1. You read this advertisement on the Internet about learning French in a language school in Montpellier.

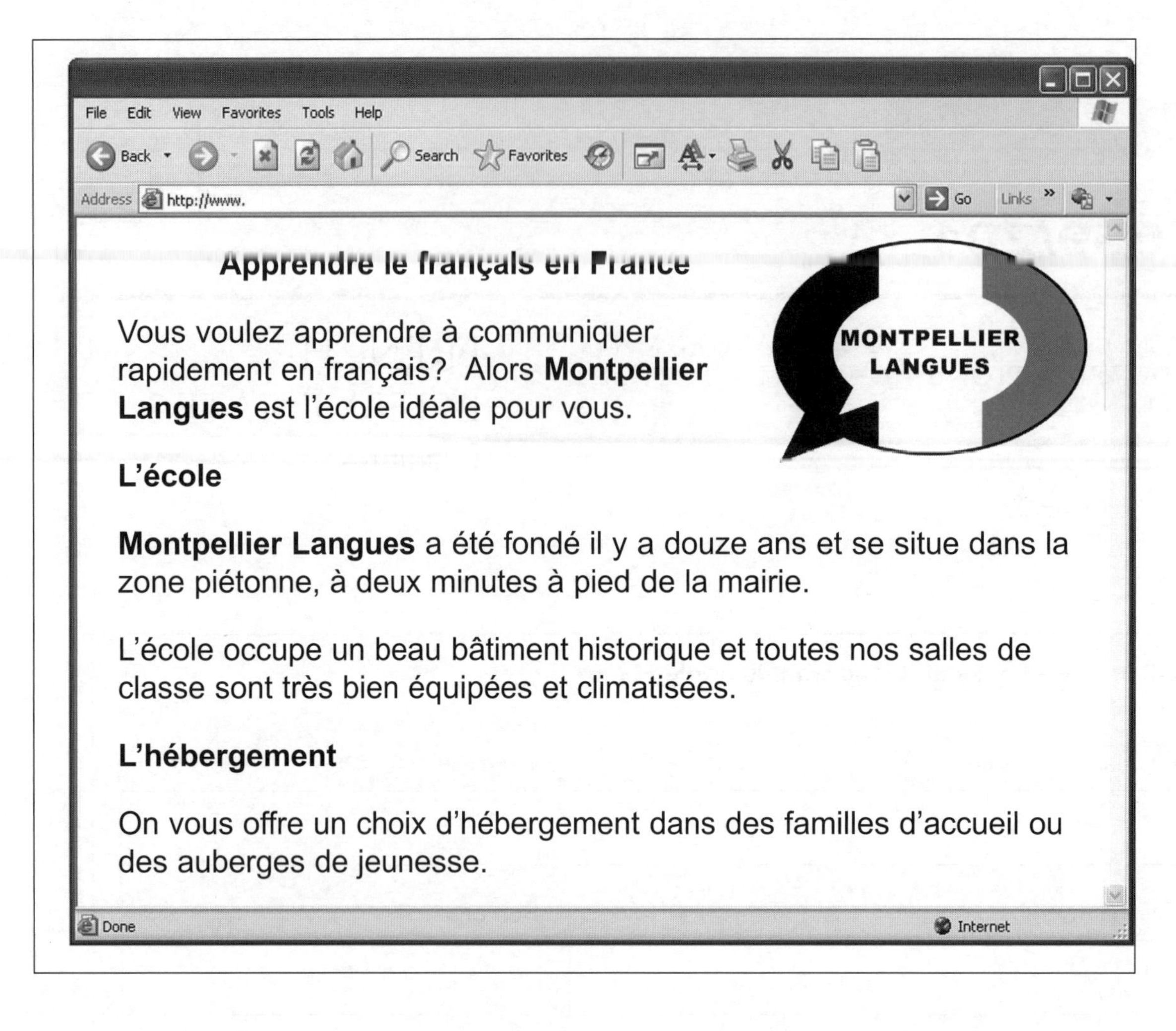

(*a*) When was the school founded? **1**

____

(*b*) Where in Montpellier is the school situated? Mention any **one** thing. **1**

____

(*c*) What are the classrooms like? Mention **two** things. **2**

____

____

(*d*) What type of accommodation does the school offer? Mention any **one** thing. **1**

____

DO NOT WRITE IN THIS MARGIN

Marks

2. You are interested and you read on to find out more about the lessons.

PROGRAMME DES COURS

Les cours

Les cours ont lieu tout au long de l'année sauf les jours fériés et ils commencent toujours le lundi. Ils se font en petits groupes et pendant les cours du matin les étudiants travailleront l'écoute, la lecture et l'écrit.

L'après-midi les étudiants auront l'occasion de pratiquer la langue dans des situations réelles, par exemple: appeler la gare SNCF pour se renseigner sur les horaires, acheter des produits frais au marché, prendre rendez-vous chez le médecin etc.

(*a*) Complete the sentence. **1**

Lessons take place all year except ______________________________.

(*b*) What will the students work on during the morning lessons? Mention any **two** things. **2**

____

____

(*c*) In the afternoons, the students will have the opportunity to practise their French in real life situations. Give any **two** examples. **2**

____

____

[Turn over

DO NOT WRITE IN THIS MARGIN

Marks

3. You read an article in a French magazine about the summer holidays.

Les vacances scolaires, sont-elles pour se reposer?

A la fin de l'année scolaire, il est souvent très difficile de s'adapter aux vacances. Il est important que les élèves prennent le temps de se détendre, et de voir des copains.

Mais en réalité beaucoup de jeunes continuent à étudier pendant les vacances, surtout ceux qui ont été malades pendant l'année scolaire.

D'autres gagnent de l'argent en tondant les gazons et en promenant les chiens des voisins pour s'acheter un nouvel ordinateur ou se payer des vacances à l'étranger.

(*a*) What is it important for pupils to do once they are on holiday? Mention any **one** thing. **1**

____

(*b*) Why do some pupils continue to study during the holidays? **1**

____

(*c*) What do some young people do to earn money? **2**

____

____

(*d*) What do they do with the money they earn? Mention any **one** thing. **1**

____

[Turn over for Question 4 on *Pages six, seven* and *eight*

4. You then find an article about relationships between grandparents and grandchildren.

Les grands-parents! Ça passe ou ça casse?

Lorsqu'on est petit, on adore aller chez ses grands-parents pour passer une journée au bord d'un lac et jeter du pain aux canards. Mais en grandissant on préfère sortir en boîte avec des copains plutôt que de jouer aux jeux de société avec des personnes âgées.

Sandrine nous parle de ses relations avec ses grands-parents

Quand j'étais petite, je voyais mes grands-parents tous les mardis soirs car je n'avais pas d'école le mercredi. Je m'amusais bien chez eux. Ils vivent près de la mer, alors le matin on faisait des châteaux de sable et le soir ils me lisaient une histoire pour m'endormir.

Mais les choses ont changé dès que je suis entrée au lycée. Ma grand-mère a commencé à me critiquer tout le temps. Elle n'aime pas la façon dont je m'habille, les bijoux que je mets et elle dit que je suis trop jeune pour porter du maquillage. Quant à mon grand-père, il me traite comme si j'avais toujours huit ans.

Mes parents et moi leur rendons visite une fois par semaine et nous passons les fêtes ensemble mais ce n'est pas comme avant. J'espère qu'en vieillissant je me rapprocherai d'eux à nouveau.

Marcel nous parle de ses relations avec ses petits-enfants.

J'ai soixante-douze ans et j'ai perdu ma femme il y a cinq ans. Heureusement, j'ai deux filles et quatre petits-enfants merveilleux. Ils me rendent visite au moins trois fois par semaine et ils m'aident avec le ménage et le jardin.

Sophie, ma petite-fille de onze ans, m'apprend à utiliser mon ordinateur. Grâce à son aide, je peux faire mes courses sur Internet et aussi communiquer avec mon neveu qui habite aux Etats-Unis.

Quand j'étais jeune, mes grands-parents étaient plutôt strictes. Par exemple, à table je devais me tenir droit sur ma chaise et ne jamais interrompre les conversations. De plus, je n'aurais jamais osé leur parler de mes goûts musicaux.

Moi au contraire, je suis beaucoup plus détendu avec mes petits-enfants. J'adore parler des choses qui les intéressent et leur donner des conseils quand ils ont des problèmes. Vivent les jeunes!

DO NOT WRITE IN THIS MARGIN

Marks

4. (continued)

(*a*) According to the article we love going to our grandparents when we are young. What do we like doing with them? Mention any **one** thing. **1**

Sandrine speaks about her relationship with her grandparents.

(*b*) Why did Sandrine go to her grandparents on Tuesday evenings? **1**

(*c*) (i) What did they do together in the morning? **1**

(ii) What did her grandparents do in the evening? **1**

(*d*) Sandrine says things have changed.

(i) Why does her grandmother criticise her now? Mention any **two** things. **2**

(ii) How does her grandfather treat her? **1**

(*e*) What does she hope will happen when she gets older? **1**

Marcel speaks about his relationship with his grandchildren.

(*f*) What do his grandchildren help him with? Mention **two** things. **1**

[turn over to page eight for questions 4(*g*) to 4(*i*)

DO NOT WRITE IN THIS MARGIN

Marks

4. (continued)

(*g*) He speaks about his granddaughter Sophie.

(i) What does she do for him? **1**

____

(ii) Thanks to her help, what can he do now? **2**

____

____

(*h*) Marcel says that his grandparents were strict. Mention any **two** examples he gives to show this. **2**

____

____

(*i*) What examples does he give to show that he is more relaxed with his grandchildren? Mention any **one** thing. **1**

____

Total (30)

[*END OF QUESTION PAPER*]

X059/203

NATIONAL QUALIFICATIONS 2011

TUESDAY, 17 MAY
10.30 AM – 11.00 AM
(APPROX)

FRENCH
INTERMEDIATE 2
Listening Transcript

This paper must not be seen by any candidate.

The material overleaf is provided for use in an emergency only (eg the recording or equipment proving faulty) or where permission has been given in advance by SQA for the material to be read to candidates with additional support needs. The material must be read exactly as printed.

©

Transcript—Intermediate 2

Instructions to reader(s):

For each item, read the English **once**, then read the French **three times**, with an interval of 1 minute between the three readings. On completion of the third reading, pause for the length of time indicated in brackets after each item, to allow the candidates to write their answers.

Where special arrangements have been agreed in advance to allow the reading of the material, those sections marked **(f)** should be read by a female speaker and those marked **(m)** by a male; those sections marked **(t)** should be read by the teacher.

(t) While in France, you are listening to the radio.

Question number one.

You hear a talk by Jérôme, whose class has helped Harona, who lives in Cameroon in Africa.

You now have one minute to study the question.

(m) **Bonjour, je m'appelle Jérôme et j'ai seize ans. Je suis élève au lycée franco-allemand dans le sud-ouest de l'Allemagne près de la frontière suisse. Notre prof de géographie a proposé à ma classe d'aider un enfant dans un pays pauvre. Nous avons contacté une organisation qui aide les enfants dans les pays en difficulté. Nous avons discuté pendant un mois et finalement nous avons choisi le Cameroun parce qu'on y parle français et nous pouvons ainsi écrire nos lettres en cours de français. Depuis juin dernier, nous correspondons avec un jeune camerounais, Harona, qui a 12 ans et qui habite un petit village où on parle français. Tous les mois, nous vendons des gâteaux à l'école pendant la récréation. Cet argent aide son village à acheter des vêtements et des médicaments. Nous voulons aussi offrir à Harona un appareil-photo avec lequel il pourra prendre des photos qu'il peut nous envoyer. Comme ça, nous pourrons mieux apprécier comment ils vivent dans son village. Nous espérons continuer cette amitié pendant longtemps.**

(2 minutes)

(t) **Question number two.**

You then hear a programme about circuses in France.

You now have one minute to study the question.

(m) or (f) **Le cirque est aujourd'hui moins populaire en France qu'il y a cinquante ans. Mais pendant l'été on voit toujours des affiches pour les cirques dans chaque ville, dans chaque petit village. C'est un monde magique, pour les enfants et leurs parents – un monde de musique, de lumières et de couleurs. Mais le cirque moderne a beaucoup changé. Par exemple, maintenant il y a beaucoup de cirques sans animaux sauvages. Dans le cirque moderne il y a beaucoup de disciplines telles que la danse. Mais tout a l'air d'être organisé comme l'était le cirque d'autrefois, surtout quand le cirque se déplace d'une ville à l'autre. Les gens du cirque se lèvent très tôt le matin, afin d'éviter les embouteillages et d'arriver à leur nouvel emplacement le plus rapidement possible. Une fois arrivés, ils prennent le déjeuner, et ils font une petite sieste avant le spectacle de l'après-midi à 14h 30. Quand celui-ci se termine, ils ont juste le temps de ranger leur matériel et de manger avant le spectacle du soir qui commence à 19h 30. Heureusement, il y a des villes où ils restent plusieurs jours. Ils en profitent pour faire les magasins ou se promener un peu en ville.**

(2 minutes)

(t) Question number three.

You then hear an interview with 14-year old Laura who lives and works with her family in a circus.

You now have one minute to study the question.

(f) Salut! Je m'appelle Laura et j'ai 14 ans. J'habite dans une caravane avec mes parents et mon frère. Je suis contente car j'ai ma propre chambre où je peux jouer aux jeux vidéos. Mon père fait un spectacle avec des chevaux et ma mère est acrobate. Le matin avant d'aller à l'école, j'aide mon père à soigner les chevaux. Ils sont mignons – petits et blancs. J'ai aussi d'autres tâches. Par exemple je vends des glaces pendant l'entracte et je répare les costumes. Avant, je devais aller dans une nouvelle école à chaque fois que le cirque bougeait. J'avais des difficultés à m'adapter car les matières étaient souvent différentes et je n'avais pas toujours le temps de me faire des amis. Mais maintenant mon école est dans le cirque. Il y a un seul professeur qui voyage avec nous et les enfants de tous les âges sont ensemble dans la même classe. Et j'aime bien être avec les autres enfants du cirque. On est très proches car on vit et on travaille ensemble.

(2 minutes)

(t) End of test.

Now look over your answers.

[*END OF TRANSCRIPT*]

[BLANK PAGE]

FOR OFFICIAL USE

Mark

X059/202

NATIONAL QUALIFICATIONS 2011

TUESDAY, 17 MAY
10.30 AM – 11.00 AM
(APPROX)

FRENCH
INTERMEDIATE 2
Listening

Fill in these boxes and read what is printed below.

Full name of centre

Town

Forename(s)

Surname

Date of birth
Day Month Year

Scottish candidate number

Number of seat

When you are told to do so, open your paper.

You will hear three items in French. **Before you hear each item, you will have one minute to study the question.** You will hear each item three times, with an interval of one minute between playings, then you will have time to answer the questions about it before hearing the next item.

Write your answers, **in English**, in this book, in the appropriate spaces.

You may take notes as you are listening to the French, but only in this book.

You may **not** use a French dictionary.

You are not allowed to leave the examination room until the end of the test.

Before leaving the examination room you must give this book to the Invigilator. If you do not, you may lose all the marks for this paper.

©

DO NOT WRITE IN THIS MARGIN

Marks

While in France, you are listening to the radio.

1. You hear a talk by Jérôme, whose class has helped Harona, who lives in Cameroon in Africa.

(*a*) In which part of Germany does Jérôme live? Mention any **one** thing. **1**

(*b*) Who suggested that his class should help someone in a poor country? **1**

(*c*) Why did they choose to help someone in Cameroon? Mention any **one** thing. **1**

(*d*) What age is Harona? **1**

(*e*) How do the pupils raise money for their project? **1**

(*f*) What does the money buy? Mention any **one** thing. **1**

(*g*) Why do they want Harona to send them photos? **1**

* * * * *

DO NOT WRITE IN THIS MARGIN

Marks

2. You then hear a programme about circuses in France.

(*a*) What makes the circus "a magical world"? Mention any **two** things. **1**

(*b*) In what ways has the modern circus changed? **2**

(*c*) Why do circus workers have to get up early when they move from town to town? Mention any **one** thing. **1**

(*d*) What do they do when they arrive in a new town? Mention any **one** thing. **1**

(*e*) What is the time of the evening performance? **1**

(*f*) What can they do if they stay in town for a few days? Mention any **one** thing. **1**

* * * * *

[Turn over for Question 3 on *Page four*

DO NOT WRITE IN THIS MARGIN

Marks

3. You then hear an interview with 14-year old Laura who lives and works with her family in a circus.

(*a*) Why does Laura like her bedroom? Mention any **one** thing. **1**

(*b*) How does she help her father? **1**

(*c*) What other tasks does Laura do in the circus? Mention any **one** thing. **1**

(*d*) Why did Laura find it difficult always having to change schools? Mention **two** things. **2**

(*e*) Her school is now in the circus. Why does she like this new arrangement? Mention any **one** thing. **1**

* * * * *

Total (20)

[*END OF QUESTION PAPER*]

X059/204

NATIONAL QUALIFICATIONS 2011

TUESDAY, 17 MAY
11.20 AM – 12.00 NOON

FRENCH INTERMEDIATE 2
Writing

20 marks are allocated to this paper.

You may use a French dictionary.

You are preparing an application for the job advertised below.

Titre de Poste	:	Vendeur/Vendeuse au rayon vêtements
Profil	:	Conseiller les clients, organiser les rayons
Renseignements	:	Pour plus de détails, contactez: **M. Le Roux,** Chef du rayon Prêt-à-porter Carrefour 34000 Montpellier

To help you to write your application, you have been given the following checklist of information to give about yourself and to ask about the job. Make sure you deal with **all** of these points:

- name, age, where you live
- leisure interests
- school/college career – subjects studied previously/being studied now
- reasons for application
- request for information about the job.

You could also include the following information:

- any previous links with France or a French-speaking country
- work experience, if any.

You have also been given a way to start and finish this formal type of letter:

Formal opening to letter of application

Monsieur/Madame/Messieurs,

Suite à votre annonce, je me permets de poser ma candidature pour le poste de . . .

Formal finish to letter of application

En espérant que ma demande retiendra votre attention, je vous prie d'accepter, Monsieur/Madame/Messieurs, l'expression de mes sentiments distingués.

Use all of the above to help you write **in French** the letter which should be 120–150 words, excluding the formal phrases you have been given. You may use a French dictionary.

[*END OF QUESTION PAPER*]

INTERMEDIATE 2

2012

[BLANK PAGE]

FOR OFFICIAL USE

Mark

X059/11/01

NATIONAL QUALIFICATIONS 2012

THURSDAY, 24 MAY 9.00 AM – 10.10 AM

FRENCH INTERMEDIATE 2
Reading

Fill in these boxes and read what is printed below.

Full name of centre

Town

Forename(s)

Surname

Date of birth

Day Month Year

Scottish candidate number

Number of seat

When you are told to do so, open your paper and write your answers **in English** in the spaces provided.

You may use a French dictionary.

Before leaving the examination room you must give this book to the Invigilator. If you do not, you may lose all the marks for this paper.

©

DO NOT WRITE IN THIS MARGIN

Marks

1. While on the Internet, you read about a competition to win a trip to the Christmas market in Lille.

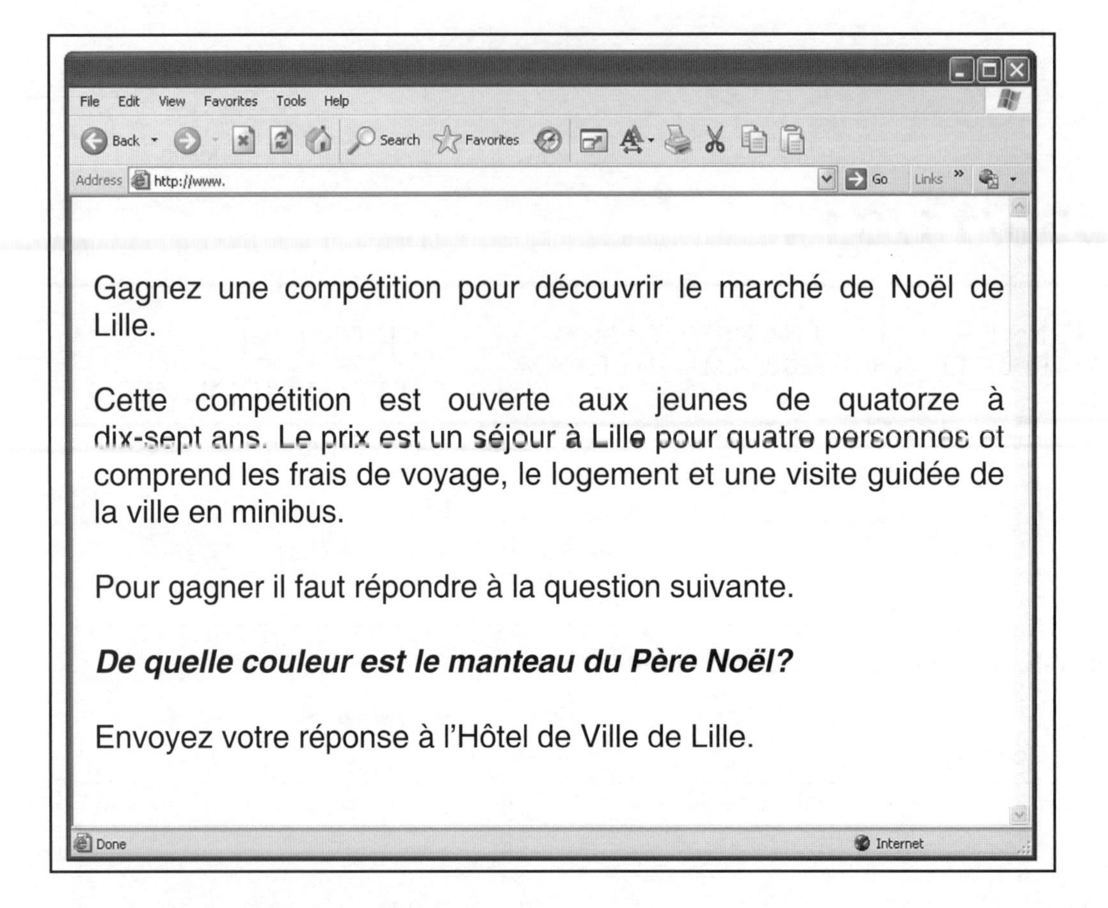

(*a*) Complete the following sentence. **1**

The competition is open to young people between the ages of ________

and ________.

(*b*) What does the trip include? Mention any **two** things. **2**

____

____

(*c*) What question must you answer to win? **1**

____

(*d*) Where do you have to send your answer? **1**

____

DO NOT WRITE IN THIS MARGIN

Marks

2. You are interested and you want to find out more about the Christmas market.

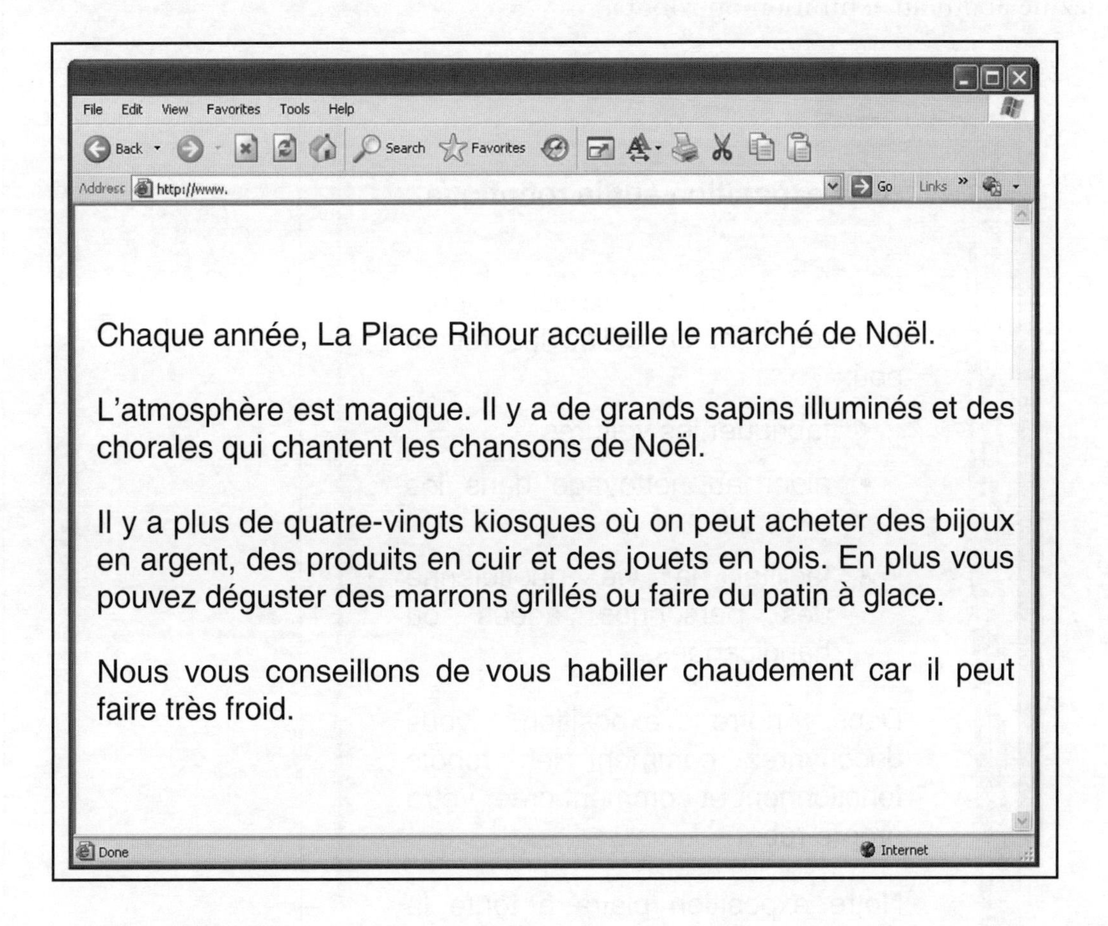

Chaque année, La Place Rihour accueille le marché de Noël.

L'atmosphère est magique. Il y a de grands sapins illuminés et des chorales qui chantent les chansons de Noël.

Il y a plus de quatre-vingts kiosques où on peut acheter des bijoux en argent, des produits en cuir et des jouets en bois. En plus vous pouvez déguster des marrons grillés ou faire du patin à glace.

Nous vous conseillons de vous habiller chaudement car il peut faire très froid.

(*a*) Why is the atmosphere at the market described as magical? Mention any **one** thing. **1**

(*b*) What can you buy from the kiosks? Mention any **two** things. **2**

(*c*) What else can you do at the market? Mention any **one** thing. **1**

(*d*) What are you advised to do? **1**

[Turn over

DO NOT WRITE IN THIS MARGIN

Marks

3. You win the competition and go to Lille. While there, you read an article in a magazine about an exhibition on robots.

Une exposition sur la robotique.

Venez visiter notre exposition pour voir comment on utilise les robots pour:

- fabriquer les voitures
- aider au nettoyage dans les hôpitaux
- faciliter la vie quotidienne des personnes âgées ou handicapées.

Dans notre exposition vous découvrirez comment les robots fonctionnent et comment créer votre propre robot.

Notre exposition plaira à toute la famille, car elle offre quelque chose pour tous les goûts.

(*a*) Mention any **two** examples of how we use robots. **2**

____

____

(*b*) What will you discover at the exhibition? Mention **two** things. **2**

____

____

(*c*) Why will all the family enjoy the exhibition? **1**

____

[Turn over for Question 4 on *Pages six, seven and eight*

4. While in France you read an article about the increase in reality TV programmes.

Depuis quelques années la télé-réalité est devenue très populaire. Mais qui profite vraiment de ces émissions – les participants, le public ou les producteurs ?

Deux personnes nous donnent leur avis.

Nadine 21 ans

Moi, j'adore la télé réalité. Quand j'allume la télé je n'ai pas envie de réfléchir et je veux me détendre après une longue journée de travail.

Mon émission préférée est «Secret Story». Je trouve intéressant de voir comment les participants s'entendent entre eux et comment les relations entre les gens se développent.

Au début, les gens qui participent dans ces programmes sont des étrangers mais après quelques jours je me sens très proche d'eux. En fait, ils finissent par faire partie de ma vie. Par exemple, j'en parle tout le temps au boulot avec mes collègues ou au café autour d'un verre avec mes vrais amis et puis à la fin de la semaine il faut absolument que je vote pour mon favori pour qu'il évite l'éviction.

A mon avis, la télé-réalité offre à tout le monde une chance de réussir dans le monde des médias. Même moi, j'ai déjà fait une demande pour faire partie d'une émission dans laquelle on cherche le plus beau mannequin de la France.

Maurice 28 ans

Pour moi, la télévision est un outil très important pour s'informer et s'instruire.

Cela dit, je comprends pourquoi la télé-réalité est très populaire car ça donne la possibilité au public de choisir les vedettes de demain.

Par contre, je trouve les émissions de réalité inutiles et très dangereuses. Elles donnent de faux espoirs aux participants qui ont souvent des difficultés à s'adapter à la célébrité ou à retrouver une vie normale.

Je trouve vraiment injuste la facilité avec laquelle ces inconnus deviennent célèbres. Moi, je suis musicien professionnel et j'ai dû travailler dur pour être connu. En plus, il y a maintenant beaucoup d'acteurs et de chanteurs qui ont du mal à trouver du travail et qui se retrouvent souvent au chômage à cause de ces émissions.

A mon avis, ces programmes ne produisent pas des gens créatifs mais des marionnettes manipulées par des producteurs gourmands.

DO NOT WRITE IN THIS MARGIN

Marks

4. (continued)

(*a*) What question is asked about reality TV in the opening paragraph? **1**

Nadine gives her opinion about reality TV.

(*b*) Why does Nadine love reality TV? Mention any **one** thing. **1**

(*c*) What does she find interesting about "Secret Story"? Mention any **one** thing. **1**

(*d*) In what ways do the contestants become part of her life? **3**

(*e*) What reality programme has Nadine applied for? **1**

Maurice gives his opinion about reality TV.

(*f*) Why does Maurice think television is an important tool? Mention any **one** thing. **1**

(*g*) According to Maurice, what makes reality television so popular? **1**

DO NOT WRITE IN THIS MARGIN

Marks

4. (continued)

(*h*) Why does he think reality TV is dangerous? Mention any **two** things. **2**

(*i*) What does he find unfair about these programmes? **3**

(*j*) What is his final opinion about these programmes? Mention any **one** thing. **1**

Total (30)

[*END OF QUESTION PAPER*]

X059/11/12

NATIONAL QUALIFICATIONS 2012

THURSDAY, 24 MAY
10.30 AM – 11.05 AM
(APPROX)

FRENCH
INTERMEDIATE 2
Listening Transcript

This paper must not be seen by any candidate.

The material overleaf is provided for use in an emergency only (eg the recording or equipment proving faulty) or where permission has been given in advance by SQA for the material to be read to candidates with additional support needs. The material must be read exactly as printed.

Transcript—Intermediate 2

Instructions to reader(s):

For each item, read the English **once**, then read the French **three times**, with an interval of 1 minute between the three readings. On completion of the third reading, pause for the length of time indicated in brackets after each item, to allow the candidates to write their answers.

Where special arrangements have been agreed in advance to allow the reading of the material, those sections marked **(f)** should be read by a female speaker and those marked **(m)** by a male; those sections marked **(t)** should be read by the teacher.

(t) During your trip to Lille, you meet a French girl called Valérie.

Question number one.

She tells you about her holiday in Spain.

You now have one minute to study the question.

(f) **Bonjour je m'appelle Valérie et j'ai 18 ans. Il y a deux mois, mes parents m'ont emmenée en vacances en Espagne. C'était super. On avait une grande maison sur trois étages à 10 minutes du centre ville. J'avais ma propre chambre avec un balcon qui donnait sur le jardin et la mer. Pendant la première semaine j'ai pris des cours d'espagnol dans une école de langues. Les cours duraient de 9 heures à 13 heures. Puis, l'après-midi, l'école organisait des activités culturelles. Par exemple, on a pratiqué des danses traditionnelles et on a visité des villages typiques de l'Espagne. La deuxième semaine, on avait plus de temps libre. Un jour on a pris le bateau pour aller au Maroc. Quel beau pays! Je garde un bon souvenir des grandes maisons, des belles plages et des marchés en plein air. Les Marocains étaient vraiment accueillants et c'était un grand avantage qu'ils parlent français car on a pu se comprendre. Je me suis tellement amusée que je compte y retourner avec mes amis pendant les grandes vacances.**

(2 minutes)

(t) **Question number two.**

While in Lille you eat in a famous restaurant which has just won an award. At the end of the meal you meet Jean, the head chef, who tells you about himself and his career.

You now have one minute to study the question.

(m) **Bonjour, je m'appelle Jean. Je suis chef cuisinier depuis 11 ans et je viens de gagner le prix du meilleur restaurant traditionnel de Lille. Mais je n'ai pas toujours voulu être chef. Quand j'étais enfant, je voulais être vétérinaire car je vivais dans une ferme et j'aidais mon père à s'occuper des animaux. Et puis, un jour, j'ai été forcé d'apprendre à cuisiner. Ma mère devait passer deux semaines à l'hôpital et comme mon père lui rendait visite tous les jours, je devais faire à manger pour mes petits frères. J'ai tout de suite adoré cuisiner et depuis, la cuisine est ma passion. Par contre, le travail de chef est dur. Je dois me lever très tôt le matin pour faire la préparation et je travaille souvent 15 heures par jour. Mais mon travail a de bon côtés. J'adore travailler avec mon équipe et inventer de nouvelles recettes, mais le mieux est d'avoir la satisfaction de voir mes clients revenir régulièrement. Je suis très heureux d'avoir reçu ce prix et je remercie toute mon équipe et tous mes clients pour leur soutien.**

(2 minutes)

(t) **Question number three.**

While in Lille you listen to the radio. You hear about problems there have been because of the bad weather.

You now have one minute to study the question.

(m) or (f) **Bonsoir à tous. Voici les infos sur Radio 4. Il y a eu beaucoup de problèmes dans le nord de la France à cause du mauvais temps. Dans la journée d'hier 20 cm de neige sont tombés et par conséquent beaucoup de maisons se retrouvent sans eau ni électricité. Les aéroports ont dû annuler certains vols et beaucoup d'écoles ont fermé. Ce mauvais temps a aussi rendu les routes très dangereuses et hier soir, il y a eu un accident sur la Route Nationale 3. L'accident est arrivé vers 18 heures quand trois voitures et une moto sont entrées en collision. Heureusement personne n'a été gravement blessé. Météo France annonce de la neige pour les jours à venir. Il est donc conseillé de ne pas sortir sauf en cas de nécessité. Si vous devez prendre la voiture, il est recommandé de se renseigner sur l'état des routes avant tout départ, de prendre un thermos de boisson chaude et d'avoir un téléphone portable en cas d'urgence.**

(2 minutes)

(t) **End of test.**

Now look over your answers.

[*END OF TRANSCRIPT*]

[BLANK PAGE]

FOR OFFICIAL USE

Mark

X059/11/02

NATIONAL QUALIFICATIONS 2012

THURSDAY, 24 MAY
10.30 AM – 11.05 AM (APPROX)

FRENCH INTERMEDIATE 2
Listening

Fill in these boxes and read what is printed below.

Full name of centre

Town

Forename(s)

Surname

Date of birth
Day Month Year

Scottish candidate number

Number of seat

When you are told to do so, open your paper.

You will hear three items in French. **Before you hear each item, you will have one minute to study the question.** You will hear each item three times, with an interval of one minute between playings, then you will have time to answer the questions about it before hearing the next item.

Write your answers, **in English**, in this book, in the appropriate spaces.

You may take notes as you are listening to the French, but only in this book.

You may **not** use a French dictionary.

You are not allowed to leave the examination room until the end of the test.

Before leaving the examination room you must give this book to the Invigilator. If you do not, you may lose all the marks for this paper.

©

PB X059/11/02 6/10110

DO NOT WRITE IN THIS MARGIN

Marks

During your trip to Lille, you meet a French girl called Valérie.

1. She tells you about her holiday in Spain.

(*a*) She describes the house in which she was staying. Tick (✓) the **two** correct statements. **2**

The house had three floors.	
The house was in the centre of town.	
Her bedroom was clean.	
She had a balcony overlooking the garden.	

(*b*) During the first week, Valérie had Spanish lessons. What time did the lessons start **and** finish? **1**

____

(*c*) What type of cultural activities did the school offer in the afternoon? Mention any **one** thing. **1**

____

(*d*) What memories does she have of Morocco? Mention any **two** things. **2**

____

____

(*e*) She says the Moroccans were very welcoming. What other advantage does she mention? **1**

____

* * * * *

DO NOT WRITE IN THIS MARGIN

Marks

2. While in Lille you eat in a famous restaurant which has just won an award. At the end of the meal you meet Jean, the head chef, who tells you about himself and his career.

(*a*) For how long has Jean been a chef? **1**

(*b*) Why did he want to be a vet when he was younger? Mention any **one** thing. **1**

(*c*) What happened that forced Jean to learn how to cook? Mention any **one** thing. **1**

(*d*) He says that being a chef is hard. What **two** examples does he give of this? **2**

(*e*) What does he love about his job? Mention any **two** things. **2**

* * * * *

[Turn over for Question 3 on *Page four*

DO NOT WRITE IN THIS MARGIN

Marks

3. While in Lille you listen to the radio. You hear about problems there have been because of the bad weather.

(*a*) What disruption has been caused because of the bad weather? Mention any **two** things. **2**

(*b*) There is also news of a road accident.

(i) At what time did the accident take place? **1**

(ii) What vehicles were involved? Mention **two** things. **1**

(*c*) If you need to go out in the car, what are you advised to do? Mention any **two** things. **2**

* * * * *

Total (20)

[*END OF QUESTION PAPER*]

X059/11/03

NATIONAL QUALIFICATIONS 2012

THURSDAY, 24 MAY
11.25 AM – 12.05 PM

FRENCH
INTERMEDIATE 2
Writing

20 marks are allocated to this paper.

You may use a French dictionary.

You are preparing an application for the job advertised below.

Titre du Poste	:	Réceptionniste au Musée
Profil	:	Accueillir et conseiller les clients, savoir parler l'anglais et le français
Renseignements	:	Pour plus de détails, contactez **Mme Martin** Musée d'Art Contemporain 34 Rue d'Enghien **59000 Lille**

To help you write your application, you have been given the following checklist of information to give about yourself and to ask about the job. Make sure you deal with **all** of these points:

- name, age, where you live
- leisure interests
- school/college career—subjects studied previously/being studied now
- reasons for application
- request for information about the job.

You could also include the following information:

- any previous links with France or a French-speaking country
- work experience, if any.

You have also been given a way to start and finish this formal type of letter:

Formal opening to letter of application

> Monsieur / Madame / Messieurs,
>
> Suite à votre annonce, je me permets de poser ma candidature pour le poste de . . .

Formal finish to letter of application

> En espérant que ma demande retiendra votre attention, je vous prie d'accepter, Monsieur / Madame / Messieurs, l'expression de mes sentiments distingués.

Use all of the above to help you write **in French** the letter which should be 120–150 words, excluding the formal phrases you have been given. You may use a French dictionary.

[*END OF QUESTION PAPER*]

INTERMEDIATE 2

2013

[BLANK PAGE]

FOR OFFICIAL USE

Mark

X059/11/01

NATIONAL QUALIFICATIONS 2013

WEDNESDAY, 29 MAY
9.00 AM – 10.10 AM

FRENCH
INTERMEDIATE 2
Reading

Fill in these boxes and read what is printed below.

Full name of centre

Town

Forename(s)

Surname

Date of birth
Day Month Year

Scottish candidate number

Number of seat

When you are told to do so, open your paper and write your answers **in English** in the spaces provided.

You may use a French dictionary.

Before leaving the examination room you must give this book to the Invigilator. If you do not, you may lose all the marks for this paper.

DO NOT WRITE IN THIS MARGIN

Marks

1. You want to work in France during the holidays. You see this advert on the Internet.

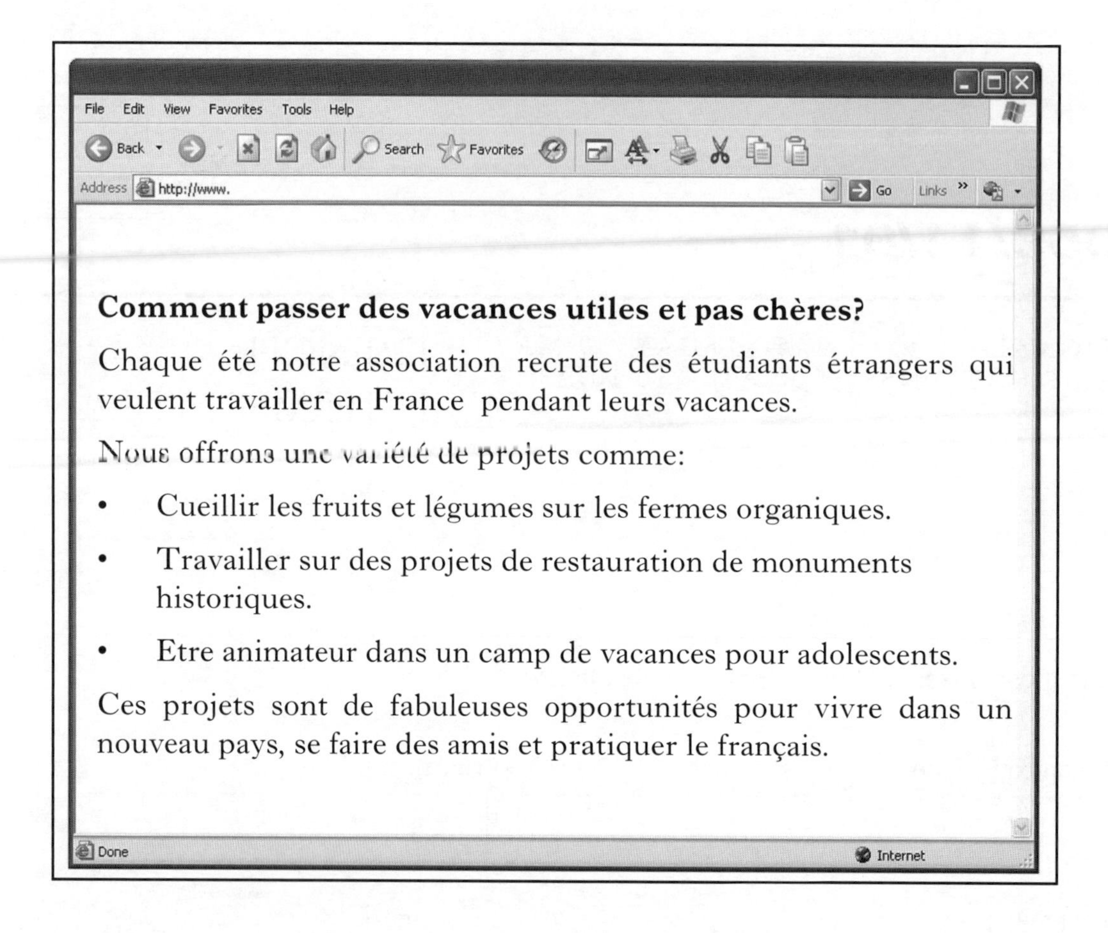

(*a*) What type of people does the association recruit? **1**

____

(*b*) Give any **two** examples of projects they could do. **2**

____

____

(*c*) What opportunities do these projects offer? Mention any **two** things. **2**

____

____

DO NOT WRITE IN THIS MARGIN

Marks

2. You are interested in a project based in the village of Germolles and go on to find out more.

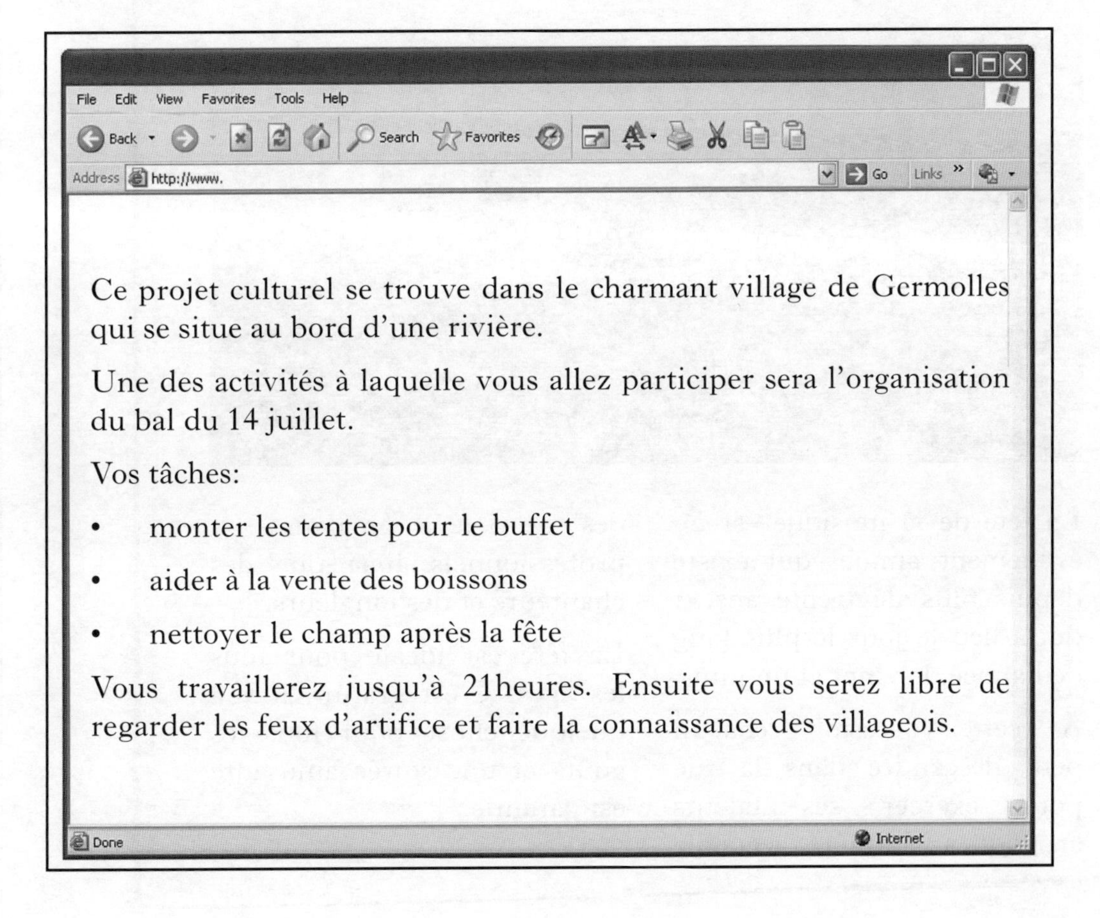

Ce projet culturel se trouve dans le charmant village de Germolles qui se situe au bord d'une rivière.

Une des activités à laquelle vous allez participer sera l'organisation du bal du 14 juillet.

Vos tâches:

- monter les tentes pour le buffet
- aider à la vente des boissons
- nettoyer le champ après la fête

Vous travaillerez jusqu'à 21heures. Ensuite vous serez libre de regarder les feux d'artifice et faire la connaissance des villageois.

(*a*) Where is the village of Germolles situated? **1**

(*b*) Mention any **two** tasks you will have to carry out. **2**

(*c*) What will you be free to do when you have finished working? Mention **two** things. **2**

[Turn over

DO NOT WRITE IN THIS MARGIN

3. While in France you read an article about the annual music festival. *Marks*

La fête de la musique est un événement annuel qui existe depuis plus de trente ans et qui a lieu le jour le plus long de l'année, le vingt et un juin.

A cette occasion chacun peut descendre dans la rue pour exercer ses talents artistiques. La fête accueille des musiciens amateurs ou professionnels ainsi que des chanteurs et des jongleurs.

La fête est idéale pour tous les âges. C'est gratuit, il y a quelque chose pour tous les goûts et une soirée amusante est garantie.

(*a*) For how long has the music festival existed? **1**

____

(*b*) When does it take place? **1**

____

(*c*) Complete the sentence.

The festival welcomes amateur and professional musicians as well as **1**

____________________ and ____________________.

(*d*) Why is the festival ideal for people of all ages? Mention any **two** things. **2**

____

____

[Turn over for Question 4 on *Pages six, seven and eight*

4. You read another article in a magazine.

Introduction

C'est votre dernière année au lycée et la réussite aux examens est très importante. Mais vous arrivez aussi à l'âge où il vous est possible de trouver un petit emploi.

Est-il possible d'obtenir le bon équilibre entre études et travail?

Deux jeunes gens nous donnent leur avis.

Sophie

Quand j'avais 16 ans mes parents ont décidé de supprimer mon argent de poche et donc, j'étais obligée de trouver un petit boulot. J'ai vu une annonce dans la vitrine d'un magasin de vêtements pour un poste de vendeuse et j'y travaille maintenant tous les samedis.

Au début c'était difficile de gérer mon temps entre le travail et les études. Alors, j'ai dû apprendre à organiser mon emploi du temps—je passe mon dimanche entièrement à étudier et deux heures chaque soir à faire mes devoirs.

J'aime mon travail car ça m'a donné plus de confiance en moi-même. Je suis devenue plus mûre et en plus, je gagne mon propre argent. Le seul inconvénient est que je suis trop fatiguée pour sortir en semaine.

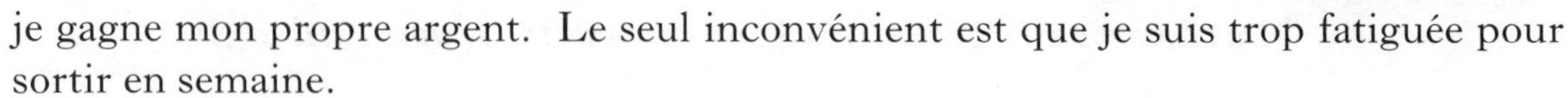

Christian

Je ne crois pas que les jeunes devraient travailler en même temps qu'étudier. On devrait profiter de sa jeunesse avant de passer sa vie à travailler. Aussi, comme il y a tant de chômeurs, il est injuste de donner un emploi à un étudiant.

A mon avis, il est très important de consacrer du temps à ses études. La réussite aux examens offre plus d'options pour l'avenir. Par exemple, on a plus de chance d'étudier à l'université de son choix, de faire un apprentissage professionnel et de trouver un premier emploi.

A mon avis, il y a d'autres moyens d'acquérir un peu d'expérience de la vie. Moi, par exemple, je fais partie d'une association pour les jeunes du quartier. On organise des randonnées à cheval en campagne, des pièces de théâtre et des boums pour les anniversaires. D'accord, je ne suis pas payé mais en étant membre d'une telle association, j'ai appris à travailler au sein d'une équipe et à communiquer avec des gens de tous milieux.

DO NOT WRITE IN THIS MARGIN

Marks

4. (continued)

(*a*) What question is being asked in the introduction? **1**

Sophie

(*b*) What did Sophie's parents do when she was 16? **1**

(*c*) How did she find a job? **1**

(*d*) She says she had to learn how to organise her study time. How does she do this? Mention **two** things. **2**

(*e*) Why does she like her job? Mention any **two** things. **2**

(*f*) What is the only disadvantage she mentions? **1**

Christian

(*g*) Why does Christian think young people should not work and study at the same time? Mention **two** things. **2**

(*h*) Christian thinks that success in exams can improve your options in the future. What does he say about this? Mention any **two** details. **2**

DO NOT WRITE IN THIS MARGIN

Marks

4. (continued)

(*i*) Christian helps out with a local youth organisation. What kind of activities do they organise? Mention any **two**. **2**

(*j*) What has Christian learned by being part of this association? Mention any **one** thing. **1**

Total (30)

[*END OF QUESTION PAPER*]

X059/11/12

NATIONAL QUALIFICATIONS 2013

WEDNESDAY, 29 MAY 10.30 AM – 11.05 AM (APPROX)

FRENCH INTERMEDIATE 2
Listening Transcript

This paper must not be seen by any candidate.

The material overleaf is provided for use in an emergency only (eg the recording or equipment proving faulty) or where permission has been given in advance by SQA for the material to be read to candidates with additional support needs. The material must be read exactly as printed.

©

Transcript—Intermediate 2

Instructions to reader(s):

For each item, read the English **once**, then read the French **three times**, with an interval of 1 minute between the three readings. On completion of the third reading, pause for the length of time indicated in brackets after each item, to allow the candidates to write their answers.

Where special arrangements have been agreed in advance to allow the reading of the material, those sections marked **(f)** should be read by a female speaker and those marked **(m)** by a male; those sections marked **(t)** should be read by the teacher.

(t) You are helping with the preparations for the festival in the village of Germolles.

Question number one.

While you are there, you meet Cédric who has worked there before.

You now have one minute to study the question.

(m) Bonjour, je m'appelle Cédric. Ça fait deux ans maintenant que j'aide à la préparation de cette fête à Germolles. Par contre l'année dernière la fête a été annulée. Il y avait de gros orages et il a plu pendant une semaine entière, ce qui est vraiment rare en été. C'était vraiment dommage mais on a pu repousser la fête au 30 juillet. J'adore ce petit village car c'est tranquille, tout le monde se connaît et il y a un petit marché tous les mercredis matins. De plus, Germolles est l'endroit idéal pour les gens qui aiment faire de la photographie. Le paysage est magnifique et la lumière est parfaite. Moi, en fait, je viens d'une grande ville dans le sud de la France mais je déteste la vie urbaine. D'abord, il y a trop de bruit, puis les logements sont trop chers et pour finir on ne se sent pas en sécurité car la vie en ville peut être très dangereuse. Mon rêve est d'avoir une maison à la campagne pour vivre une vie saine et calme.

(2 minutes)

(t) Question number two.

While in France you listen to the radio. Mélanie, a Canadian girl, is talking about her sporting career.

You now have one minute to study the question.

(f) Bonjour, je m'appelle Mélanie et je suis canadienne. Je suis nageuse et j'ai commencé à faire de la natation sérieusement quand j'avais 9 ans avec le club de l'école. A l'âge de 14 ans j'avais déjà gagné quelques médailles et j'ai été choisie pour faire partie de l'équipe nationale du Canada. Pour rester à ce niveau il faut que je m'entraîne très dur. Je passe au moins 4 heures par jour dans la piscine et donc je n'ai pas beaucoup de temps libre. Mais quand j'ai le temps j'aime promener mes deux chiens, cuisiner ou tout simplement écouter de la musique. Malgré tout l'entraînement que je fais, je n'ai pas pu participer aux Jeux Olympiques de Londres l'année dernière car je me suis cassé le bras en faisant du ski. J'espère, par contre, être en pleine forme pour les Jeux du Commonwealth qui auront lieu à Glasgow l'an prochain. Je ne suis jamais allée en Grande Bretagne et après les jeux, je voudrais profiter de l'occasion pour visiter l'Ecosse, déguster les plats traditionnels écossais et améliorer mon anglais.

(2 minutes)

(t) Question number three.

Mélanie goes on to talk about an event she is holding to persuade young people to lead a healthier life.

You now have one minute to study the question.

(f) Je suis aussi venue en France pour persuader les enfants de mener une vie plus saine en devenant plus actifs. D'après les statistiques, la santé des jeunes devient de plus en plus problématique. Ceci est dû principalement à 2 choses. Les jeunes passent trop de temps assis devant l'ordinateur et ils ne mangent pas à des heures régulières. En fait, ils grignotent toute la journée. Ceci est très inquiétant. Alors quoi faire? Pour commencer, je crois que les parents devraient encourager leurs enfants à faire au moins trente minutes d'exercice physique par jour et les supermarchés devraient faire des promotions sur les fruits et les légumes et non pas sur les chips et le chocolat. Pour ma part, j'ai décidé d'organiser une journée active le premier août dans toutes les grandes villes de France et du Canada. Il y aura beaucoup d'activités amusantes et sportives comme la danse, le tennis de table et la voile. De plus, il y aura des sportifs célèbres qui seront prêts à parler aux parents et à signer des autographes. Je vous encourage tous à nous rejoindre et pour en savoir plus, consultez notre site. Merci à tous et à très bientôt j'espère.

(*2 minutes*)

(t) End of test.

Now look over your answers.

[*END OF TRANSCRIPT*]

[BLANK PAGE]

FOR OFFICIAL USE

Mark

X059/11/02

NATIONAL QUALIFICATIONS 2013

WEDNESDAY, 29 MAY
10.30 AM – 11.05 AM (APPROX)

FRENCH
INTERMEDIATE 2
Listening

Fill in these boxes and read what is printed below.

Full name of centre

Town

Forename(s)

Surname

Date of birth
Day Month Year

Scottish candidate number

Number of seat

When you are told to do so, open your paper.

You will hear three items in French. **Before you hear each item, you will have one minute to study the question.** You will hear each item three times, with an interval of one minute between playings, then you will have time to answer the questions about it before hearing the next item.

Write your answers, **in English**, in this book, in the appropriate spaces.

You may take notes as you are listening to the French, but only in this book.

You may **not** use a French dictionary.

You are not allowed to leave the examination room until the end of the test.

Before leaving the examination room you must give this book to the Invigilator. If you do not, you may lose all the marks for this paper.

©

DO NOT WRITE IN THIS MARGIN

Marks

You are helping with the preparations for the festival in the village of Germolles.

1. While you are there, you meet Cédric who has worked there before.

(*a*) Why was the festival cancelled last year? Mention any **one** thing. **1**

____

(*b*) On what date did it eventually take place? **1**

____

(*c*) Why does Cédric love the village of Germolles? Mention any **two** things. **2**

____

____

(*d*) Why does he say Germolles is ideal for people who like photography? Mention any **one** thing. **1**

____

(*e*) Cédric lives in a big city. What does he not like about city life? Mention any **two** things. **2**

____

____

* * * * *

DO NOT WRITE IN THIS MARGIN

Marks

2. While in France you listen to the radio. Mélanie, a Canadian girl, is talking about her sporting career.

(*a*) How old was Mélanie when she took up swimming seriously? **1**

(*b*) What had happened to her by the time she was 14 years old? Mention any **one** thing. **1**

(*c*) What does she like doing in her free time? Mention any **two** things. **2**

(*d*) Why was she not able to take part in the Olympic Games in London last year? **1**

(*e*) She hopes to compete in the Commonwealth Games next year. What does she want to do after the Games? Mention any **two** things. **2**

* * * * *

[Turn over for Question 3 on *Page four*

DO NOT WRITE IN THIS MARGIN

Marks

3. Mélanie goes on to talk about an event she is holding to persuade young people to lead a healthier life.

(*a*) The health of young people is becoming more problematic. Why is this? Mention **two** things. **2**

____

____

(*b*) According to Mélanie what should be done? Complete the sentences. **2**

Parents should encourage their children to ______________________________

____.

Supermarkets should ______________________________

____.

(*c*) Mélanie is organising a "get active day". What kind of activities will there be? Mention any **two**. **1**

____

____

(*d*) There will be some famous sports personalities there. What will they be prepared to do? Mention any **one** thing. **1**

____

* * * * *

Total (20)

[*END OF QUESTION PAPER*]

X059/11/03

NATIONAL QUALIFICATIONS 2013

WEDNESDAY, 29 MAY
11.25 AM – 12.05 PM

FRENCH
INTERMEDIATE 2
Writing

20 marks are allocated to this paper.

You may use a French dictionary.

You are preparing an application for the job advertised below.

Titre du Poste	:	Serveur/Serveuse dans un café
Profil	:	prendre les commandes des clients, servir à manger et à boire
Renseignements	:	Pour plus de détails, contactez **M. LACROIX** **Café de la Paix** **66400 ST JEAN DE CORTS**

To help you to write your application, you have been given the following checklist of information to give about yourself and to ask about the job. Make sure you deal with **all** of these points:

- name, age, where you live
- leisure interests
- school/college career—subjects studied previously/being studied now
- reasons for application
- request for information about the job

You could also include the following information:

- any previous links with France or a French-speaking country
- work experience, if any

You have also been given a way to start and finish this formal type of letter:

Formal opening to letter of application

> Monsieur / Madame / Messieurs,
>
> Suite à votre annonce, je me permets de poser ma candidature pour le poste de . . .

Formal finish to letter of application

> En espérant que ma demande retiendra votre attention, je vous prie d'accepter, Monsieur / Madame / Messieurs, l'expression de mes sentiments distingués

Use all of the above to help you write **in French** the application, which should be 120–150 words, excluding the formal phrases you have been given. You may use a French dictionary.

[*END OF QUESTION PAPER*]

INTERMEDIATE 2 | ANSWER SECTION

ANSWER SECTION FOR

SQA INTERMEDIATE 2 FRENCH 2009–2013

FRENCH INTERMEDIATE 2 READING 2009

1. (*a*) The Eurostras organisation is looking for students aged between **14** and **20**.

   (*b*) *Any one from:*
   - March/Next March/from March

   OR
   - Next year/this coming year

   (*c*) In a youth hostel/in youth hostels

   (*d*)
   - Make/design/draw a (small) poster/a notice
   - Explain why your school should/deserves to/must participate/take part/should be chosen

2. (*a*) *Any one from:*
   - Introduce/present themselves in French

   OR
   - Meet/talk with the other participants/meet the others/contestants

   (*b*) *Any two from:*
   - Food
   - Flags
   - Post cards

   (*c*) (i) It is made of/constructed from glass
   (ii) Talk about/discuss/debate European/EU politics/policy

   (*d*) (The one) able to/can collaborate/work best in a team/best teamwork/whose team worked the best/the best working team

3. (*a*)
   - Walked in/around the roads/streets/walked around town
   - Bought souvenirs/presents/gifts for his family

   (*b*) *Any one from:*
   - They/the groups had/there was a party/celebration/they celebrated

   OR
   - They sang songs in every/all/different/each/their own language

   (*c*) He had to say goodbye to/he was leaving/parting from/losing his new friends/the friends he had made

   (*d*) Created/made/built a garden in their school

4. (*a*) *Any two from:*
   - What am I going to do/will I do after school?/when I leave school?
   - Where am I going to/will I live/stay?
   - Am I going to/will I find a job?

   (*b*) *Any two from:*
   - He has his own room
   - His room is on the ground/bottom floor
   - His room is well equipped/equipt/has everything you need

   (*c*) *Any one from:*
   - He had to share them/it (with the other students)

   OR
   - He had to wait a long time (to get washed)/students took a long time (to shower)

   (*d*) (i) She washed (his) clothes/did (his) laundry/washing/linen
   (ii) Cooked/made (him) good/nice meals/food

   (*e*) *Any one from:*
   - He made (some) friends/he got friends

   OR
   - Went out more/started to go out (with friends)

   (*f*) (i) He gives/does/teaches/runs/takes Spanish lessons/courses/classes
   (ii) *Any two from:*
   - The rent/to pay for his flat
   - The bills/invoices
   - Leisure/free-time/spare-time (activities)/hobbies

   (*g*) *Any one from:*
   - You learn how to manage/organise/look after (your) money
   - You have more freedom/liberty/independence

   (*h*) *Any one from:*
   - He would(n't) eat correctly/properly/well/the correct/right food
   - He would get lost in a (big) city/town

   (*i*) *Any one from:*
   - He calls/phones her/she hears from him once a week/every week
   - He gives her news/he tells her the news/she gets all the news once a week/every week

   (*j*) It is (very) important to like/to love the place/area you are going to live (for a few years)/to make sure you like it first

FRENCH INTERMEDIATE 2 LISTENING 2009

1. (*a*) *Any one from:*
   - (In the centre of) Geneva (any recognisable spelling)

   OR
   - Switzerland

   (*b*)
   - It is (a bit) difficult
   - The teacher is (very) boring/the teachers are boring/the teacher doesn't make it interesting

   (*c*) *Any two from:*
   - (It) helps her to relax/it is relaxing/calming/lets out her stress
   - (It) helps her lose/get away from/forget/not to think about her problems
   - she can draw/design for the/does artwork/painting for the school magazine

   (*d*) *Any one from:*
   - Family problem(s)/problem(s) at home/family issues

   OR
   - How to get better/good grades/marks (in school)

   (*e*)
   - Impoverished/poor children('s charity/association) children in poverty/children from a poor background

2. (*a*) Two weeks/15/14 days/a fortnight

   (*b*) (i) Her friend had forgotten/didn't bring his/her/their passport/couldn't find her/his passport

   (ii) (Because of the) fog/mist

   (*c*) *Any one from:*
   - It was dirty/not clean/had not been cleaned

   OR
   - It had no fridge

   (*d*) *Any one from:*
   - (Went) swimming/swam in the pool/went in the pool
   - Played cards on the terrace/patio

   (*e*) *Any two from:*
   - She fell off (the bike)
   - She broke her leg/fractured her leg
   - She had to go to/went/ended up in hospital/they took her to hospital

3. (*a*) 3 am/3 in the morning/at night

   (*b*) *Any two from:*
   - Clothes/cloths/clothing

   OR
   - Computers

   OR
   - Alcohol/booze/drink

   (*c*)
   - They were wearing jeans, a black **jumper(s)/pullover(s)/sweater/jersey** and **white** trainers.

   (*d*) *Any one from:*
   - In a green lorry/van/truck

   OR
   - (Through/out/by the) (underground) car park/parking lot/the car park exit

   OR
   - (Through/out/by the) basement

   (*e*)
   - 03-88-20-**54-16**.

FRENCH INTERMEDIATE 2 WRITING 2009

Task

Letter of application for a job abroad, including information specified in a number of bullet points.

Assessment Process

1. With reference to *Content, Accuracy* and *Language Resource*, the overall quality of the response will be assessed and allocated to a pegged mark.
2. All 5 unavoidable bullet points should have been addressed. (There are 7 bullets, 2 of which include the words 'if any' and will not incur penalties if omitted.)
3. 2 marks (ie single marks, not pegged ones) will be deducted for each bullet not addressed, up to a maximum of 2 bullets. If 3 or more bullets have not been addressed, the mark must be 0.

(See answers to 2009 Writing paper on pages 111–112 for descriptions of marking categories and responses to 'What if..?' questions.)

What if....? *(instructions for markers)*

- *The candidate has failed to copy out the introductory section or has not adapted it to the correct gender?*
  Pay minimal attention to this. However, it is an initial indication that the candidate probably will not attain the top mark.
- *Three bullet points fit into one category but two others are in the next, lower category?*
  This is often an indication that you would award the higher category.
  However, it may be wise to consider which bullet points are better. If the better sections include the first and second bullet points, which are more basic, you are less likely to be generous than if the final bullet points were of a better quality. You must look carefully at the quality of the candidate's work and then come to a decision. When in doubt give the candidate the benefit of the doubt.
- *The candidate very clearly is applying for an entirely different job to the one on the examination paper?*
  The maximum award which can be given is 8/20, if the language is considered to be worth 12 or more.
  If the language is assessed at 8, award the mark 4.
  Otherwise, award 0.

Category/mark	*Content*	*Accuracy*	*Language Resource – Variety, Range, Structures*
Very Good 20	• All five compulsory areas are covered fully, in a balanced way, including some complex sentences. • Candidates cover the initial bullet points very correctly and competently but also provide detailed information in response to the later bullet points, which are specific to the job advert in question. • A range of verbs/verb forms, tenses and constructions is used. • Overall this comes over as a competent, well thought-out and serious application for a job.	• The candidate handles all aspects of grammar and spelling accurately, although the language may contain 1 or 2 minor errors. • Where the candidate attempts to use language more appropriate to Higher, a slightly higher number of inaccuracies need not detract from the overall very good impression.	• The candidate is comfortable with the first person of the verb and generally uses a different verb or verb form in each sentence. • Some modal verbs and infinitives may be used, especially at Bullet Point (BP) 5. • There is good use of tenses, adjectives, adverbs and prepositional phrases and, where appropriate, word order. • The candidate uses co-ordinating conjunctions and/or subordinate clauses, especially from BP 3. • The language flows well.
Good 16	• All five compulsory tasks are addressed, perhaps mainly using less complex sentences. • The responses to bullet points 4 and 5 may be thin, although earlier points are dealt with in some detail. • The candidate uses a reasonable range of verbs/verb forms.	• The candidate handles verbs accurately but simply. • There are some errors in spelling, adjective endings and, where relevant, case endings. • Use of accents is less secure. • Where the candidate is attempting to use more complex vocabulary and structures, these may be less successful, although basic structures are used accurately. • There may be one or two examples of inappropriately selected vocabulary, especially in the later bullet points.	• There may be repetition of verbs. • Where relevant, word order is simple. • There may be examples of listing, in particular at BP 3, without further amplification. • There may be one or two examples of a co-ordinating conjunction, but most sentences are simple sentences. • The candidate keeps to more basic vocabulary and structures in the final two bullet points and may only ask for one piece of information eg How much will I earn?
Satisfactory 12	• The candidate uses mainly simple, basic sentences. • The language is fairly repetitive and uses a limited range of verbs and fixed phrases, eg *I like*; *I go*; *I play*. • Area 4 (reasons for application) may be covered in a rather vague manner. • Area 5 (questions) may be addressed either with a general question or one single specific question, frequently about money or time off.	• The verbs are generally correct, but basic. • There are quite a few errors in other parts of speech - gender of nouns, cases, singular/plural confusion. • Prepositions may be missing eg I go the town. • While the language may be reasonably accurate in the first three areas, in the remaining two control of the language structure may deteriorate significantly. • Overall, there is more correct than incorrect.	• The candidate copes with the first and third person of a few verbs. • A limited range of verbs are used on a number of occasions. • Sentences are basic and mainly brief. • There is minimal use of adjectives, probably mainly after 'is' eg Chemistry is interesting. • The candidate has a weak knowledge of plurals. • There may be several spelling errors eg reversal of vowel combinations.

Category and mark	*Content*	*Accuracy*	*Language Resource – Variety, Range, Structures*
Unsatisfactory 8	• The content is basic. • The language is repetitive, eg *I like, I go, I play* may feature several times within one area. • As far as content is concerned, there may be little difference between Satisfactory and Unsatisfactory. • While the language used to address BP 1 and 2 is reasonably accurate, serious errors appear during BP 3.	• Ability to form tenses is inconsistent. • There are errors in many other parts of speech - gender of nouns, cases, singular/plural confusion. • Several errors are serious, perhaps showing mother tongue interference. • There may be one sentence which is not intelligible to a sympathetic native speaker. • The final two areas may be very weak. • Overall, there is more incorrect than correct.	• The candidate copes mainly only with the personal language required at BP 1 and 2. • The verbs 'is' and 'study' may also be used correctly. • Sentences are basic. • An English word may appear in the writing. • There may be an example of serious dictionary misuse.
Poor 4	• The content and language are very basic.	• Many of the verbs are incorrect. • There are many errors in other parts of speech - personal pronouns, gender of nouns, cases, singular/plural confusion. • Prepositions are not used. • The language is probably inaccurate throughout the writing. • Three or four sentences may not be understood by a sympathetic native speaker.	• The candidate cannot cope with more than 1 or 2 basic verbs. • The candidate displays almost no knowledge of the present tense of verbs. • Verbs used more than once may be written differently on each occasion. • Sentences are very short. • The candidate has a very limited vocabulary. • Several English words may appear in the writing. • There are examples of serious dictionary misuse.
Very Poor 0	• The content is very basic **or** • The candidate has not completed at least three of the core bullet points.	• (Virtually) nothing is correct. • Most of the errors are serious. • Very little is intelligible to a sympathetic native speaker.	• The candidate copes only with 'have' and 'am'. • Very few words are correctly written in the foreign language. • English words are used. • There may be several examples of mother tongue interference. • There may be several examples of serious dictionary misuse.

FRENCH INTERMEDIATE 2 READING 2010

1. (*a*)
- Twins
- 12 years old

(*b*) *Any one from:*
- Leaving for/Going to US(A), America next year

or
- To speak/talk (English) with the children/help the children with English

(*c*)

Your bedroom must be kept clean	
You will have the main bedroom	
Your bedroom is next to the children's	✓
You will have to share the bathroom	✓

2. (*a*)
- Every day except Wednesday and Sunday/not on Wednesday and Sunday

(*b*)
- Help with homework
- Look after/occupy/be in charge of/entertain them/keep them busy when/if the parents go out/we go out

(*c*) *Any one from:*
- Ironing
- Help to prepare/make (the) meals/food/cooking

(*d*) *Any one from:*
- French lesson(s)/course(s)/class(es)
- Look around/walk in the neighbouring/nearby areas/districts/neighbourhood/quarter

3. (*a*)
- The language/French is spoken (everywhere)/ The main language is French/The majority speak French
- Historic buildings/dating from that time

(*b*) *Any one from:*
- Sun(ny)(practically) all year/always/all the time/every year
- Warm welcome (from the people)/friendly people/population/welcoming

(*c*) *Any two from:*
- Beautiful coast(line)/the coast is/the coasts are beautiful
- Traditional fishing villages
- Busy/Lively towns/cities

4. (*a*) *Any one from:*
- To forget work/studies/school
- To get away/escape from everyday/daily life/get a break from their normal life

(*b*) *Any one from:*
- Split up with boyfriend
- Was ill (for a few months)

(*c*)
- Spain for a week (**need both parts**)

(*d*) *Any two from:*
- Relax/rest/unwind
- Read
- Get a tan/sunbathe

(*e*) *Any two from:*
- Too many people/tourists/too busy
- No room/place for her towel/nowhere to put her towel/nowhere to sit
- Got (painful) sunburn/sunstroke/heat stroke/too much sun

(*f*) *Any two from:*
- Food was bad/not good/not nice
- Couldn't sleep because of noise (from nightclubs)/ noise kept her awake/because of the nightclub
- Mosquito(es) biting/stinging her

(*g*) *Any one from:*
- (Afraid) to leave the house empty/no-one to look after the house
- No one to water the garden/flowers

(*h*) (Read about it) in a magazine/an article

(*i*) *Any three from:*
- They have all the comfort(s) of a home/house/all mod cons
- Away from/far from tourists/there are no tourists (nearby)
- Find out about/get to know/become acquainted with/meet other families (living in the neighbourhood/nearby)/get to meet another family
- Children never get bored

(*j*) (Only) have to pay/buy the plane/flight ticket/ agency fees

FRENCH INTERMEDIATE 2 LISTENING 2010

1. (*a*) • 16

(*b*) • Same age/both 16
• Things/Lots in common/Same interests/like(d) the same things/stuff/hobbies/(both) like(d) fashion/(both) fashionable

(*c*) • (Her) family and (her) town/city/where she lives

(*d*) *Any one from:*
• Teachers are **more/very** understanding (in Great Britain)/Teachers are **less** understanding **in France**
or
• They/The pupils have **less** homework (in Great Britain)/Pupils have **more** homework **in France**

(*e*) • Played cards/a card game
or
• Talked about difference between the (two) countries/France and England/France and (Great) Britain

(*f*) • Study (foreign) languages

2. (*a*) *Any one from:*
• (Too) young/not old enough/young girl
or
• (Too) dangerous/not safe (on her own)/she could get hurt

(*b*) *Any one from:*
• She keep in touch/contact/phone/speak (to them) every day/always/all the time
or
• Help (her aunt) with the housework/chores

(*c*) *Any one from:*
(i) • She had to be in by 21:00/9 (p.m./in the evening/at night)/Was not allowed out after 9
or
• Couldn't/wasn't allowed to invite friend(s) to the house/have friend(s) round/over/stay over

(ii) • She found/leased/ rented/got/moved into/decided to stay in a flat/apartment/ house/home with (her new) (boy) friend(s)

(*d*) *Any one from:*
• Sold ice creams/ice cream seller/vendor/server
or
• Works at/a job at/on the beach/seaside

(*e*) *Any one from:*
• First experience/time without (her) parents
or
• Experience of life/real world/travelling without (her) parents
or
• (Got more/Gained/grew in) (self-)confidence

3. (*a*) • A year ago/last year

(*b*) • He worked in a nursery (school)/preschool/day care/Kindergarten/crèche
• with children between **3** and **6** years old

(*c*) *Any one from:*
• Games/play/sport(s)/play time
or
• Songs/singing/singalong

(*d*) • They were poor/didn't have a lot of/had little money/poor living conditions/can cope without money/didn't have a lot
• They were (always) smiling/happy/cheerful/ positive/live happily/have a good spirit

(*e*) • You get to know/learn about/are more aware of a country/the inhabitants
or
• About a country/how others live/what the people are like/about the inhabitants/lifestyles/what it is like to live there

FRENCH INTERMEDIATE 2 WRITING 2010

Task

Letter of application for a job abroad, including information specified in a number of bullet points.

Assessment Process

1 With reference to *Content, Accuracy* and *Language Resource*, the overall quality of the response will be assessed and allocated to a pegged mark.

2. All 5 unavoidable bullet points should have been addressed. (There are 7 bullets, 2 of which include the words 'if any' and will not incur penalties if omitted.)

3. 2 marks (ie single marks, not pegged ones) will be decucted for each bullet not addressed, up to a maximum of 2 bullets. If 3 or more bullets have not been addressed, the mark must be 0.

(See answers to 2009 Writing paper on pages 111–112 for descriptions of marking categories and responses to 'What if..?' questions.)

FRENCH INTERMEDIATE 2 READING 2011

1. (*a*) • 12 years ago

(*b*) *Any one from:*
- Pedestrian precinct/zone/area/pedestrianised zone/street
- Two minutes (on foot) from/to the town hall/ mayor's office/town house

(*c*) *Any two from:*
- Well equipped/good equipment/well fitted
- Air-conditioned/conditioning
- In a historic building

(*d*) *Any one from:*
- Host families/family/with a family
- (Youth) hostel(s)

2. (*a*) • Lessons take place all year except bank/public holidays

(*b*) *Any two from:*
- Listening
- Reading
- Writing

(*c*) *Any two from:*
- Call/phone (SNCF/train) station about (train) times/timetables/schedules/information
- Get/Buy (fresh) produce/products/food at the market
- Make/take an appointment at the doctor's/arrange to meet the doctor/try to get the doctor

3. (*a*) *Any one from:*
- (Take time) to relax/unwind/rest
- Go out with/(Take time) to see friend**s**/spend time with friend**s**

(*b*)
- (They have) been ill/unwell/sick during the year
- They have been unwell

(*c*)
- Cut/mow/do grass/lawn(s) (for neighbour)
- Walk dog(s) for neighbours

(*d*) *Any one from:*
- (Buy) (a new) computer(s)
- (Pay for) a holiday(s) abroad/foreign holiday(s)

4. (*a*) *Any one from:*
- Spend day/time at lake(side)/loch
- Throw bread to/at/for the ducks/feed the ducks

(*b*) • No school on Wednesday/the next day

(*c*) (i) • Made sand castle(s)

(ii) • Read him/**her**/tell him/**her** a story

(*d*) (i) *Any two from:*
- (Doesn't like) the way/how she dresses/clothes/fashion
- (Doesn't like) the jewellery (she wears)
- Thinks she's too young to wear make-up

(ii) • As if she were still 8 years old

(*e*) • They become closer (again)/she will still be close to them/get along better

(*f*) • Cleaning/Chores/Housework/housekeeping **and** the garden

(*g*) (i) • Teaches/shows him how to use a computer/helps him with the computer/internet

(ii)
- His shopping online/on the Internet
- Skype/Speak/communicate with his nephew in USA/America

(*h*) *Any two from:*
- (At the table) he had to sit up straight/upright/properly/sit right (on his chair)
- Never/don't interrupt/disrupt conversation(s)
- Not allowed to/never dared to speak about his tastes in music

(*i*) *Any one from:*
- (Loves) speaking about the things that interest them/their interests
- (Loves to) advise them/give advice when they have problems/helps with their problems/talks about their problems

FRENCH INTERMEDIATE 2 LISTENING 2011

1. (*a*) *Any one from:*
- South west
- Near/at/on Swiss border/Switzerland

(*b*) • Geography teacher

(*c*) *Any one from:*
- They speak French (there)/They speak the same language/It's a French country
- Can write letters in French (class)/can write in French

(*d*) • 12

(*e*) • Sell/bake cakes (during interval)/home-baking/bake sale/gateaux

(*f*) *Any one from:*
- Clothes/Cloths
- Medicine(s)/medication/medical care/medical help
- Camera (for Harona)

(*g*) • They can appreciate (better) how they live (in his/her village)/see what life is like in the village/see what the village is like/see what situation Harona is in/learn about village life

2. (*a*) *Any two from:*
- Music/musical
- Light/lighting
- Colour(s)/colourful

(*b*)
- (Many without/have) no/fewer (wild) animals (now)/there used to be animals
- (Includes other acts/disciplines such as) dance/dancing

(*c*) *Any one from:*
- (to) avoid traffic (jams)/there is a lot of traffic/the roads get busy
- (to) get/arrive there as quickly/early as possible/so they are there quicker/so they can get quickly to another town/promptly

(*d*) *Any one from:*
- Have lunch/dinner/something to eat/food/a meal
- (Have a) rest/siesta/nap/sleep

(*e*) • 19.30/7.30(pm)/half 7

(*f*) *Any one from:*
- Shop(ping)/go to the shops/buy things from the shop
- Walk/around (the town)/sightsee (around the town)/walk into town

3. (*a*) *Any one from:*
- Her own room
- She can play video games/her (games) console/ PS2/3/her room/it has video games

(*b*) • (with/looks after/cares for/grooms/cleans/brushes/feeds/prepares) horse**s**/gets horse**s** ready (for performances)

(*c*) *Any one from:*
- Sells ice cream (during interval)
- Repairs/fixes/sorts costumes

(*d*)
- Subjects/classes/lessons/work/courses (were often) different/new/difficult to adapt to subjects
- (No time) to make friends/doesn't make a lot of friends/couldn't make friends/had to make (new) friends

(e) *Any one from:*
- Only one teacher/teacher travels with them/has the same teacher/she's always in the same class
- The children/they are all together in one class/she likes being with the other children/she can be with the other children/children of all ages in her class/there are other circus kids in school
- They live and work together

FRENCH INTERMEDIATE 2 WRITING 2011

Task:
Letter of application for a job abroad, including information specified in a number of bullet points.

Assessment Process:

1. With reference to *Content, Accuracy and Language Resource*, assess the overall quality of the response and allocate it to a pegged mark.
2. Check that all 5 unavoidable bullet points have been addressed. (There are 7 bullets, 2 of which include the words "if any" and will not incur penalties if omitted.)
3. Deduct 2 marks (ie single marks, not pegged ones) for each bullet not addressed, up to a maximum of 2 bullets. If 3 or more bullets have not been addressed, the mark must be 0.

(See answers to 2009 Writing paper on pages 111–112 for descriptions of marking categories and responses to 'What if..?' questions.)

FRENCH INTERMEDIATE 2 READING 2012

1. (*a*) • The competition is open to young people between the ages of **14 and 17**

   (*b*) *Any two from:*
   - Travel (expenses)/Transport
   - Accommodation/place to stay/housing/lodging
   - A (bus) tour of the town/Lille/city (in a minibus)/ a guide of the town

   (*c*) • What colour is Father Christmas's/Santa Claus's coat/jacket/cloak?

   (*d*) • town hall/city chambers/town house

2. (*a*) *Any one from:*
   - (big) illuminated/(flood) lit (Christmas/fir) trees/trees lit up
   - Choir(s)/they/people sing(ing) Christmas songs/carols/ hymns/Christmas choirs/carol singers

   (*b*) *Any two from:*
   - silver jewellery/jewels in silver/silver jewels
   - leather product(s)/thing(s) made from leather
   - wooden toy(s)/game(s)

   (*c*) *Any one from:*
   - Eat/have/buy/sample/try/taste hot/grilled/cooked/toasted/ roasted chestnuts
   - (go) ice-skating

   (*d*) • wear warm clothes/dress warmly/wrap up warmly/dress well because it is cold

3. (*a*) *Any two from:*
   - Make/produce/build/manufacture cars
   - Cleaning in hospital(s)
   - Help old people/an old person/people with disabilities

   (*b*) • how robots work/function/the way that robots work
   • (how to) create/make a robot

   (*c*) • offers for all tastes/something for everyone/for all the family/to interest everyone/something for all ages/ something everyone will enjoy

4. (*a*) • Who gains/benefits/profits from these (programmes/reality) TV/broadcasts/this/it?
   Who doesn't really benefit?

   (*b*) *Any one from:*
   - She doesn't (want to/have to) think
   - Gives her release/loosen up/helps her relax after work/after a long day

   (*c*) *Any one from:*
   - The way/How the contestants get on (with each other)
   - The way/How (their) relations(hips) develop/you get to see the relationships between contestants

   (*d*) • She talks (about them) at work/with colleagues
   • (She talks about them when) having a drink with (real) friends/ in a café with friends
   • She votes for her favourite/to stop someone being evicted

   (*e*) • to find the most beautiful/best/top/prettiest model (in France)/mannequin

   (*f*) *Any one from:*
   - It informs/it is a source of information/you can find information/it provides information/ you can inform yourself/is informative
   - It is educational/it educates/teaches/instructs/you learn

   (*g*) • Public chooses the star(s)/celebrity(ies) (of tomorrow/ future/today)

   (*h*) • Gives false/wrong hope(s) (to participants)/gets their hopes up
   • Some find it hard to adapt to fame/celebrity/becoming a celebrity/from a normal life
   or
   to go back to/to find their normal life
   NB: only 1 mark available from second bullet point

   (*i*) • How easily/quickly/the ease/with which these people become famous/they haven't had to work hard to become famous/they become famous without working hard/they make it easier for people to become celebrities
   • He had to work (hard) to become famous/to be known
   • Many actors/singers have difficulty finding a job
   or
   Many actors/singers are unemployed
   NB: Only 1 mark available from third bullet point

   (*j*) *Any one from:*
   - They do not produce creative people/they produce marionettes/puppets/(very) uncreative people
   - They are manipulated/controlled by (greedy) producers/producers are manipulative

FRENCH INTERMEDIATE 2 LISTENING 2012

1. (*a*)

The house had three floors	✓
The house was in the centre of town	
Her bedroom was clean	
She had a balcony overlooking the garden	✓

(*b*)
- 9 (am)/9 (in the morning)
- 1300 hours/1(pm)

(*c*) *Any one from:*
- Traditional/Spanish/national/regional dance(s)
- visits to the typical/Spanish village(s)

(*d*) *Any two from:*
- Big/grand/large house(s)
- Beautiful/pretty/lovely/nice beach(es)
- open air/outdoor/outside market(s)/shopping in the open air/street market(s)
- boat trip
- (it is) a beautiful country

(*e*) *Any one from:*
- They/many/some spoke French/to speak French/an advantage
- could understand her/each other/she could understand them /they could understand French

2. (*a*) • (For) 11 years

(*b*) *Any one from:*
- Lives/Lived/worked/was brought up on a farm/his dad/they had animals/helped dad on farm
- Looked after /helped with the animals

(*c*) *Any one from:*
- Mum (had to spend two weeks) in hospital
- His dad visited her every day/often/regularly
- Had to cook for brother(s)/feed his brother(s)

(*d*)
- Has to wake up/get up/come in/prepare/work/start early in the morning
- (Often) works 15 hours a day

(*e*) *Any two from:*
- (Working with) his team/he gets to work in a team/he has a great team
- Inventing/creating (new) recipes/being creative/(making) new dishes
- Customer satisfaction/when people like his food/ customers returning/customers thank him for his food/ compliment him for his food/ satisfying his regular customers

3. (*a*) *Any two from:*
- No water/electricity/power cuts/water is off
- (lots of) schools closed
- airports (have had to cancel flights/flights cancelled)
- Roads are dangerous/icy/slippy

(*b*) (i) • 1800 hours/6pm

(ii) • (3) cars and a motorbike

(*c*) *Any two from:*
- find out about (the state of) the roads/plan your route (before you leave)
- (take) a flask/a hot/warm drink
- (have a) mobile/cell/phone/moby

FRENCH INTERMEDIATE 2 WRITING 2012

Task:

Letter of application for a job abroad, including information specified in a number of bullet points.

Assessment Process:

1. With reference to *Content, Accuracy and Language Resource*, assess the overall quality of the response and allocate it to a pegged mark.
2. Check that all 5 unavoidable bullet points have been addressed. (There are 7 bullets, 2 of which include the words "if any" and will not incur penalties if omitted.)
3. Deduct 2 marks (ie single marks, not pegged ones) for each bullet not addressed, up to a maximum of 2 bullets. If 3 or more bullets have not been addressed, the mark must be 0.

(See answers to 2009 Writing paper on pages 111–112 for descriptions of marking categories and responses to 'What if..?' questions.)

FRENCH INTERMEDIATE 2 READING 2013

1. (*a*) • foreign students/pupils/students/pupils from abroad

   (*b*) *Any two from:*
   - Pick/gather/harvest/collect fruit and vegetables (on organic farms)
   - (preserve/plan/work on) restoration project(s)/(work on) restoring old/historic monument(s)/buildings
   - Be a children's/teenagers'/youth rep/host/organiser/leader in a holiday camp/be a rep host/organiser/leader in camp for children/teenagers/youth/adolescent

   (*c*) *Any two from:*
   - life/live/work in a new/foreign/different country/land/abroad
   - make friends/meet new friends
   - perfect/improve/use/practise/speak French

2. (*a*) • on the banks of/at the sides/at/next to/close to/on the edge of/border of/on/beside a river

   (*b*) *Any two from:*
   - Assemble/raise/Put up the tents (for the buffet)
   - (Help to) sell drink(s)/serve/distribute/alcohol
   - Clear/tidy up/clean the field(s) (after the festival)

   (*c*) • (watch the) fireworks
   - Make the acquaintance of/make conversation with/get to know/meet the villagers/people from the village

3. (*a*) • (more than) 30 years

   (*b*) • Solstice/longest day of the year/21st June

   (*c*) • The festival welcomes amateur and professional musicians as well as singer(s) and juggler(s)

   (*d*) *Any two from:*
   - it is free
   - something/music for all tastes/for everyone
   - (you are guaranteed) a fun/enjoyable evening/night/evening/night entertainment/amusement(s)

4. (*a*) • Is it possible to have/obtain/maintain/get (a good) balance between school/studies and work?/is it possible to have a job and study?

   (*b*) • Take away/cut out/cut off/removed/cancelled/stopped her pocket money

   (*c*) • (She saw it)/an announcement/poster/sign/ad in a shop window/clothes shop

   (*d*) • Spends every/all day Sunday studying/revising
   - Spends two hours a night/a day on homework/studying/schoolwork

   (*e*) *Any two from:*
   - Increased/growing/more confidence/confident/trust in herself
   - Increased/growing/ more maturity/mature
   - Has her own money

   (*f*) • Too tired to go out (in the week)

   (*g*) • Enjoy their youth/they will work the rest of their life/take advantage of their youth
   - (As) there are so/too many unemployed, (it is unfair to give a job to a student)/unemployment is high

   (*h*) *Any two from:*
   - (Better chance of) studying in a university of your choice
   - (Better chance of) doing a (professional) apprenticeship
   - (Better chance of) getting your first job

   (*i*) *Any two from:*
   - Horse-riding/Pony trekking
   - (Theatre) plays/pieces/shows/dramas
   - Birthday parties/party

   (*j*) *Any one from:*
   - To be part of/to work (well) in a team/group/be a team player
   - To communicate/talk with people from different backgrounds

FRENCH INTERMEDIATE 2 LISTENING 2013

1. (*a*) *Any one from:*
   - (Big) storm(s)
   - Rained (all week)/too wet/it was flooded

   (*b*) • 30 July

   (*c*) *Any two from:*
   - Quiet/tranquil/peaceful/calm/relaxing
   - Everyone knows everyone
   - There's a (little) market(s) every Wednesday (morning)

   (*d*) *Any one from:*
   - Country(side)/landscape/setting/surroundings/scenery/ the views/it is picturesque (is magnificent)
   - Light (is perfect)/lighting

   (*e*) *Any two from:*
   - (Too) noisy/noise pollution/(too) loud
   - Lodging/accommodation/housing/rent (too) expensive
   - Don't feel safe/can/is be dangerous/life in city is dangerous

2. (*a*) • 9 (years old)

   (*b*) *Any one from:*
   - Earned/gained/won (a few) medal(s)
   - (Chosen/picked/ for) the national team/Canadian team/represented her (own) country/was in national team

   (*c*) *Any two from:*
   - Walking the dog(s)
   - Cooking
   - Listening to music

   (*d*) • Broke/injured/hurt her arm (skiing)

   (*e*) *Any two from:*
   - Visit/travel Scotland
   - Try traditional/Scottish dish(es)/food/meal(s)
   - Practise/perfect/improve/work on her English

3. (*a*) • Too much time/too long/a lot of time in front of the computer
   - Not eating at regular times/regularly/snacking all day/snack too much/too often

   (*b*) • Parents should encourage their children to do (at least) 30 minutes of (physical) exercise every day
   - Supermarkets should advertise/have promotions on/ promote/encourage people to buy/have lower prices for fruit and vegetables
     or
     not promote crisps and chocolate

   (*c*) *Any two from:*
   - Dance
   - Table tennis/ping pong
   - Sailing

   (*d*) *Any one from:*
   - Speak/talk to parents
   - Sign/give autograph(s)

FRENCH INTERMEDIATE 2 WRITING 2013

Task

Letter of application for a job abroad, including information specified in a number of bullet points.

Assessment Process

1. With reference to *Content, Accuracy* and *Language Resource*, the overall quality of the response will be assessed and allocated to a pegged mark.
2. All 5 unavoidable bullet points should have been addressed. (There are 7 bullets, 2 of which include the words 'if any' and will not incur penalties if omitted.)
3. 2 marks (ie single marks, not pegged ones) will be decucted for each bullet not addressed, up to a maximum of 2 bullets. If 3 or more bullets have not been addressed, the mark must be 0.

(See answers to 2009 Writing paper on pages 111–112 for descriptions of marking categories and responses to 'What if..?' questions.)

Acknowledgements

Permission has been sought from all relevant copyright holders and Hodder Gibson is grateful for the use of the following:
Image © Alan Heartfield/Shutterstock.com (2013 Reading page 4);
Image © Monkey Business Images/Shutterstock.com (2013 Reading page 6);
Image © Jeanne McRight/Shutterstock.com (2013 Reading page 6).